T0319002

Cambridge Elements ≡

Elements in International Relations
edited by
Jon C. W. Pevehouse
University of Wisconsin–Madison
Tanja A. Börzel
The Free University of Berlin
Edward D. Mansfield
University of Pennsylvania

WEAK STATES AT GLOBAL CLIMATE NEGOTIATIONS

Federica Genovese
University of Essex

CAMBRIDGE
UNIVERSITY PRESS

CAMBRIDGE
UNIVERSITY PRESS

University Printing House, Cambridge CB2 8BS, United Kingdom

One Liberty Plaza, 20th Floor, New York, NY 10006, USA

477 Williamstown Road, Port Melbourne, VIC 3207, Australia

314–321, 3rd Floor, Plot 3, Splendor Forum, Jasola District Centre,
New Delhi – 110025, India

79 Anson Road, #06–04/06, Singapore 079906

Cambridge University Press is part of the University of Cambridge.

It furthers the University's mission by disseminating knowledge in the pursuit of
education, learning, and research at the highest international levels of excellence.

www.cambridge.org
Information on this title: www.cambridge.org/9781108790901
DOI: 10.1017/9781108800051

First published 2020

A catalogue record for this publication is available from the British Library.

ISBN 978-1-108-79090-1 Paperback
ISSN 2515-706X (online)
ISSN 2515-7302 (print)

Additional resources for this publication at http://www.cambridge.org/genovese.

Weak States at Global Climate Negotiations

Elements in International Relations

DOI: 10.1017/9781108800051
First published online: July 2020

Federica Genovese
University of Essex
Author for correspondence: Federica Genovese, fgenov@essex.ac.uk

Abstract: This Element provides an explanation for the power of weak states in international politics, focusing on the case of international climate negotiations at the United Nations. The author points to the pitfalls of assuming that weak countries elicit power from their coordinated salience for climate issues. Contrastingly, it is argued that weak states' influence at global climate negotiations depends on the moral authority provided by strong states. The author maintains that weak states' authority is contingent on international vulnerability, which intersects broader domestic discussions of global justice, and pushes the leaders of strong countries to concede power to weak countries. New empirical evidence is shown in support of the theory.

Keywords: international negotiations, climate change, global power, cooperation, domestic politics

ISBNs: 9781108790901 (PB), 9781108800051 (OC)
ISSNs: 2515-706X (online), 2515-7302 (print)

Contents

1 Introduction

1.1 Weak States' Power at International Organizations: A Puzzle

Observers of international politics often assume that developed industrialized countries are the agenda-setters at international organizations. Widely seen as "strong" and capable, these countries are expected to determine the issues at international negotiations and settle global agreements without outside help. Along these lines, the realist school of international relations suggests that, even when other countries have strength in numbers, attempts to oppose strong states can easily fail because of their relative material capabilities (Krasner, 1991). If challenged, strong states can threaten to withdraw participation and stall the workings of international diplomats (Moravcsik, 1998). Consequently, it is commonly accepted that strong powers force the "weak" – as in states that are less materially capable and more internationally insecure than industrialized countries – to consent to multilateral agreements even when these leave the latter worse off (Garrett, 1992).

This perspective has had a long legacy. It effectively resisted challenges from those who point to the soft power "weaponry" of weak states (Finnemore & Sikkink, 1998; Nye, 2004). To date, most international relations scholars concur that the mechanisms trying to level the power relationships in world politics have not corrected imbalances, leaving a number of countries at the margins of the international system (Grant & Keohane, 2005; Ikenberry et al., 2009). Yet it is also largely understood that in several international policy areas weak states wield leverage. Some scholarship has shown that developing countries do not always need great powers to lead in order to strike global agreements (Risse et al., 1999). More recent research has argued that in several global institutions strong countries systematically cede disproportionate influence (Panke, 2010; Stone, 2011; Carnegie, 2014). Evidently, the literature is still unsettled on the roots and shapes of weak states' power in international organizations.

The essential question for researchers involved in this field is when and why weak states' international influence manifests itself. Historically, two positions have dominated this debate. For some, preoccupation with survival motivates the positions of small powers and catalyzes the strength and legitimacy of their preferences at international negotiations (Keohane, 1971; Handel, 1981). For others, the anxiety of remaining sovereign makes them more likely to subdue their preferences and bandwagon on the positions of strong states (Vital, 1967; Rothstein, 1968).[1] The contention is centered on different understandings of

---

[1] This debate is well captured in Ingebritsen et al. (2012), who recently revived the discussion on "small states" in international relations. For a classical review, see Keohane (1969).

how the domestic priorities, i.e. the *salience*, of weak states on international issues affect their probability of shaping international negotiations. For the former scholars, expressing urgency is a winning strategy. For the latter, acquiescing to the urgency of strong states' issues is more preferable. The debate remains open, in part because empirical findings are mixed. Some empirical studies suggest that weak states capitalize on their most salient issues (Slapin, 2008; Boerzel & Risse, 2010), while others indicate that expressing urgency is inconsequential (Kahler, 2013), or can even hurt weak states' positions (Briguglio, 1995; Lee, 2009).

In this Element I engage with this research agenda, seeking to contribute to the understanding of power at international negotiations. I focus on two limitations within extant scholarship that affect the current conceptualization of weak states' international influence. The first is that mainstream research largely assumes that the powerlessness of weak states is due to coordination failures (Wendt, 1994; Moravcsik, 1998) and that these countries can improve their bargaining outcomes by aligning their priorities (Mayer, 1992; Koremenos et al., 2001). I argue that this assumption overestimates the impact of the salience of weak states' interests, which in fact has ambiguous effects on their bargaining power. I contend that the salience of weak states' issues may have a meaningful efficacy on international agreements if these are also relevant *abroad* – especially if weak states' positions are deemed legitimate by audiences in strong states. I hold that domestic climate debates in industrialized countries have crucial implications for the empowerment of weak states at international negotiations.[2]

Second, I hold that the mainstream research on weak states uses a limited interpretation of "weakness," with the definition reflecting specific issue areas such as security (Leeds & Savun, 2007; O' Fordham, 2011) and trade relations (Drahos, 2003; Milner & Kubota, 2005; Davis, 2009; Carnegie, 2014). This Element widens the investigation of weak states to areas where weakness reflects existential rather than strictly economic concerns and where international bargaining is explicitly centered on moral claims. Climate change is one such under-investigated area. Given the distributional elements of international climate change agreements and the tangible divide between strong and weak states at climate negotiations, I maintain that studying global climate politics can provide important lessons about the power of weak states in various other political realms where lack of material capacity is associated with nuanced dimensions of moral influence.

---

[2] Some research has elevated the importance of domestic issue-attention drivers for global politics (Chong & Druckman, 2007). Less prominent, however, is the investigation of the effects of framing for bargaining success with a special focus on weak countries.

This Element addresses these issues by examining the influence of weak states at United Nations (UN) climate negotiations, in order to explain when and why these countries may obtain their most preferred outcomes at these global talks. I challenge the view that the domestic salience of weak states' positions determines their climate bargaining successes in a systematic way. By contrast, I contend that weak states' influence over international climate issues is linked to the domestic debates of stronger agenda-setting countries. The Element then elucidates the roles of transnational relations and moral framing in climate politics, and clarifies the sources of weak states' power in international organizations.

1.2 Weak States and Global Climate Cooperation: The Argument in Brief

Climate change is a global problem that requires multiple cross-national solutions. Industrialized countries have a major stake in international climate negotiations given the large expenses required to mitigate the levels of greenhouse gas (GHG) emissions they produce (Nordhaus, 2006; Barrett, 2007). Since the establishment of the United Nations Framework Convention on Climate Change (UNFCCC) in 1992, these countries have set expectations for global GHG reductions and institutionalized the international rules for mitigation and adaptation (Victor, 2001; Barrett & Stavins, 2003). Even in recent years, rich states remain critical at these negotiations (Parker et al., 2012). They still control international regulatory activities and funding mandates (Underdal, 2017; Urpelainen & Van de Graaf, 2018). It is also the sustained significance of strong states' interests that has supported the pessimistic view that global climate agreements are unfeasible in providing the level of decarbonization required to limit drastic climatic changes (Bernstein & Hoffmann, 2018).

Yet international climate talks continue, and global climate treaties such as the 2015 Paris Accord still rely on unanimous collective agreement. Importantly, several anecdotes indicate the crucial imprint of other countries on these negotiations. Many experts recall the emotional address of the Philippines delegation at the 2013 UNFCCC meeting, and the following global commitments in loss and damage issues (Vanhala & Hestbaek, 2016). The decision to substantively increase adaptation projects after the 2017 climate negotiations was also marked by the pressing of the host country, Fiji, and other Pacific Islands (Winkler & Depledge, 2018). These illustrations highlight how weak states' diplomatic efforts on some issues may shift international negotiation outcomes. But while these examples have captured researchers' attention in the form of case studies (see, e.g., Depledge, 2008; Betzold et al., 2012; Ward et al., 2001), there is still no overarching evidence for how and why these countries are able to obtain international concessions and settle specific agreements. Overall, little systematic work has been attempted to cross-nationally articulate and validate the power sources of conventionally weak states at global climate negotiations.

This Element seeks to fill this gap by providing a testable theoretical account for the relevance of these countries at global climate negotiations. I hold that the international climate negotiations cover many different issues that developed and less developed states divide and separately "own." This starting point is aligned to a realist interpretation of the climate negotiations in that I expect that strong states set the initial climate bargaining agenda. The premise is also consistent with institutionalist claims that strong developed states have more weight at the UNFCCC by virtue of being legally bound to GHG reduction by the initial terms of the UNFCCC convention (Najam et al., 2003; Vihma & Karlsson-Vinkhuyzen, 2011).

I maintain that the salience strong states attach to climate issues they own has an important impact on their bargaining success, because, by focusing on salient issues, developed countries' leaders retain domestic political support to reach their preferred international policy outcome (Dai, 2006). Thus, in line with previous research, I hold that strong, powerful states decide the outcomes over the issues they own based on how much they care about them.

Less powerful states have their own relevant issues at the climate negotiations, granted to them – or, as some would say, fought for (Victor, 2001) – since the installation of the UNFCCC. However, I argue that the salience that weak states attach to their issues has frail effects on their bargaining success, because these countries ultimately depend on some continuity of the negotiations to receive important international compensation (de Agueda Corneloup & Mol, 2014). Consequently, the emphasis weak states place on their most pressing positions can fail to send commitment signals that could convince the counter-bargaining part to concede.

Why would weak states then have power to decide over their more pressing issues? I claim that these countries are successful at settling agreements if the international community considers them particularly *vulnerable* to the stakes at hand, and specifically to climate risks. Put differently, I contend that, conditional on weak states' objective climate vulnerability, the more salient their positions, the more likely the attainment of bargaining outcomes closer to their preferred positions. This intuition is based on the understanding that perceptions of climate risk in foreign countries, and especially in strong states, crucially determine the moral legitimacy of weak states over their issues. Framing the issues of weak states around climate risks provides these with more weight in the eye of the international public (Vanhala & Hestbaek, 2016). It also constrains the leaders of strong states into conceding power if they want to avoid punitive naming and shaming at home (Busby, 2010; Murdie & Urpelainen, 2014). The contours of my argument are largely in line with other scholarship that points to the persuasiveness and "norm advocacy" of weak states (see, e.g., Risse et al., 1999, for the Commission on Human Rights, and Panke, 2013, in the context of UN General Assembly, among others). Differently than this literature, however, the contribution here is to shed more light on the concessions from the strong states' standpoint, in other words from the perspective of developed countries that accept to be persuaded about weak states' claims.

My argument has testable implications. First, my theory indicates that salience only unequivocally predicts bargaining power for strong states on "first world" climate issues – for example, discussions about mitigation technology and carbon pricing. Second, for weaker states' issues, such as adaptation, the theory suggests that salience explains negotiation success mainly if the championing countries are critically vulnerable to climate change. The claim is that climate vulnerability legitimizes weak states' bargaining positions because it is fundamentally associated with problems of social justice and global fairness that motivate civil movements and nongovernmental organizations (NGOs) in strong countries. By magnifying concerns of international vulnerability and framing them in the context of climate negotiations, civil society and NGOs keep strong states' leaders accountable to concessions to weak states.

1.3 The Conceptualization of Weakness in the Element

Given the cruciality of "weakness" – and "strength" – in this Element, it is critical to define weak and strong states before moving to the central elements of the argument. In international relations, these terms are sometimes associated with "small" and "great" states, which have long sought to capture the dichotomy between powerless and powerful. Yet these latter categories can be partly misleading if the spectrum one seeks to identify is only tangentially related to "size," as this may not be the key driving feature of international influence.[3]

I follow the literature that focuses on the terms "weak" and "strong" states in order to denote aspects of international status that move beyond size.

---

[3] On this point, researchers have found that small states often have relatively high per capita income and more political stability than other states (Easterly & Kraay, 2000).

Accordingly, "weak" states are countries of varying size which are objectively vulnerable (Handel, 1981). These are not necessarily states with low governmental control (Fukuyama, 2004) but rather states with "external" insecurity relative to self-dependent countries (Rothstein, 1968). Following this definition, weak and strong states refer, respectively, to countries that are incapable and capable of relying on their own means (Rothstein, 1968; Handel, 1981). Importantly, this categorization has political ramifications. Relative insecurity means that weak states are characterized by leaders who constantly fear for their country's survival. By contrast, strong states' leaders may not worry about their country's survival but may see their country's political direction as alterable (Keohane, 1971). Consequently, while strong states are intended as polities that are relatively insulated from other states' influence, they may well be concerned about external power in view of domestic audience costs and internal political punishment (Tomz, 2007).

To be sure, the definition of weak and strong states still has composite meaning and is still largely aligned with the categories of "small" and "great" powers, in that weak states tend to be more economically and demographically delicate than strong states. Nonetheless, "weakness" can be more nuanced in that it calls for defining criteria beyond pure economic or military fragility. In particular, the definition of "weak state" seems useful for areas of international politics such as global climate change, where state capacity has multidimensional interpretations.

With respect to climate change, "weakness" can be useful to capture aspects of *environmental vulnerability*, which is so prominent in the climate politics literature (Javeline, 2014; Busby, 2016; Betzold & Weiler, 2017). Climate vulnerability usually refers to a bundle of risks generated by the interplay between geography, poverty, and resource management. On the one hand, it assumes some resilience (or lack thereof) related to economic resources. On the other hand, it is also defined as high exposure to geology-related events such as hurricanes and typhoons, as well as dependence on climate-sensitive sectors such as natural resource extraction and rain-fed agriculture (Bankoff et al., 2013). In this Element I adopt a broad conceptualization of vulnerability to qualify weakness. In the context of climate change, I assume that "weak states" are states that are more existentially vulnerable to climatic effects, and thus potentially more entitled to legitimate survival concerns. The opposite is true of "strong states," which are more resilient to climate events overall.

This conceptualization of weak and strong states is important for my argument. It suggests that there are tangible indicators of climate risk – for example, historical exposure and geographic predisposition to climatic events – that can distinguish states at international climate negotiations. Additionally, and precisely because of a reliance on objective indicators of climate risk, this definition of strength and weakness implies that there is a vulnerability *spectrum*, and not just mere "blocks" of weak and strong countries (Vital, 1967). Along these lines, weak states represent a broader category than just developing countries. For example, emerging economies that are geographically exposed (e.g., islands or long-coast regions) are at high risk of climate change, and thus highly vulnerable to issues related to climate policies.

Last but not least, a fluid definition of weak and strong states is relevant because international climate negotiations have been historically poised by an institutional distinction between developed states listed in the first Annex of the UNFCCC (also called *"Annex I"* countries) and the developing (*"Non-Annex I"*) states. While some studies suggest that Non-Annex I countries are the most climate vulnerable states in the world (Najam et al., 2003; Kasa et al., 2008), increasingly scholars have highlighted how these categories are unproductive for a useful analysis of influence at the UNFCCC, not least because the Annexes are increasingly fragmented (Betzold et al., 2012; Bodansky, 2012). In concordance with the latter view, I hold that pegging state strength to placement on the Annex I is limitative. For example, the Non-Annex I includes groups such as the Least Developing Countries (LDC), the Alliance of Small Islands and States (AOSIS), and the Organization of the Petroleum Exporting Countries (OPEC), all of which possess different aspects of environmental sensitivity and, unsurprisingly, have historically diverged on positions at the climate negotiations. I claim that, instead of membership in the Annexes and other "simple dichotomies" (Lachapelle & Paterson, 2013), climate vulnerability indicators are more usefully associated with informative variation in preferences for climate change action. Furthermore, thinking of weakness in the form of climate vulnerability helps concentrate on the normative advocacy underlying international climate politics more than the Annex division can. I contend that the normative debates around vulnerability are crucial for understanding the systematic bursts of political success of some weak states at international climate negotiations.

1.4 Plan of Discussion

This Element argues that the international moral case made for countries at risk of climate disasters empowers weak states to win agreements on their salient issues at climate negotiations. My focus here is on the UNFCCC, the largest official body meant to address GHG emissions across the world. Studying weak states' behavior and success at the UNFCCC is insightful because, as with other UN institutions, agreements are settled with unanimity rule, which is

known to generate specific dynamics of compromise and distributive concessions (Underdal, 1980; Steinberg, 2002; Schneider, 2011). Furthermore, like
in other international organizations, the agenda at the UNFCCC is known to
be multidimensional, with some issues pivoting toward the interests of strong
states and others more in tune with the interest of weak states (Sprinz & Weiss,
2001; Victor, 2006). These features are critical for the argument put forward in
the following pages.

The Element is structured as follows. In Section 2, I expand the theoretical
framework at hand. I start from the understanding that policy issues discussed at
international climate negotiations can be divided according to those (on average) more relevant to strong states and weak states, respectively. I articulate
the reasons why emphasizing the urgency of preferred issues may or may not
help achieve ideal outcomes for the two sets of countries. Zooming in on weak
states, I present an argument for why the role of salience in shaping bargaining
success at the UNFCCC can be ambivalent, and thus why internal motivation
and domestic mobilization may not go far in explaining weak states' influence
over international climate agreements. I then propose an alternate explanation
for weak states' success that relies on foreign sources of moral legitimacy of
weak states' issues. I explain how weak states elicit power when their issues
are associated to climate change vulnerability. I then explore how these associations are embedded in domestic debates in strong countries and how they
might compel strong countries to concede power to weak ones.

In Section 3, I present the data used to evaluate the main hypothesis that,
while strong states can rely on their salience to move bargaining outcomes
toward their ideal preferences, for weak states salience only matters in a context
where they are perceived to be highly vulnerable to climate change. Testing this hypothesis requires empirical measurements of national preferences,
salience, and agreements across the issues discussed at international climate
negotiations. I describe the dataset of national positions and international agreements on climate change issues used for these purposes. The data, which were
collected for more than ninety countries at two historical climate change negotiation periods, present rich yet precise cross-national and temporal information
for the UNFCCC.

In Section 4, I show my empirical analyses. I begin by presenting two types
of research designs meant to test the core hypothesis. First, I propose to test
the effect of the interaction of a country's climate vulnerability and salience
on bargaining success using a standard regression framework. Second, I offer
an alternative approach that compares deterministic salience-based bargaining
solutions with and without climate vulnerability measures in order to evaluate
the relevance of this interaction. In the third part, I dive into the mechanisms

envisioned by the theory and provide some evidence for the sources of moral legitimacy of weak states' issues from the perspectives of strong states. Using a number of different data sources and methods, I present qualitative and quantitative evidence of the compelling role of NGOs and strong states' public opinion in associating climate vulnerability with concern for weak states and, more generally, international power redistribution. I show how global NGOs and foreign civil societies frame preferences for international concessions to weak states on the premise of climate risk.

In Section 5, I summarize the implications of the study for global climate politics research and for international relations more generally. For climate politics students, my study suggests that the power of weak states in deciding the direction of their ancillary climate change issues is driven by domestic political calculations in strong states rather than the level of urgency they convey themselves. The findings also suggest that the under-provision of optimal global climate policies – for example, with regard to adaptation, loss and damage, and forestry-specific regulation – may be in part related to an inconsistent level of moral legitimacy attached to the urgency of these issues. When associations between climate risk and weak states' survival become more clear, then climate agreements may be more internationally representative and even redistributive.

For international relations scholars more broadly, the Element proposes a new answer to the question of whether international politics is still largely driven by strong states and what role more marginal states have at international negotiations. The key argument stems from the view that strong states are still central to international organizations (Moravcsik, 1998; Schneider, 2011), but it also gives support to the proposition that weak states can credibly influence international policy decisions (Tallberg, 2010; Bayer & Urpelainen, 2013). It indicates a way in which strong states' debates affect the weight of weak states' bargaining positions, via diffusing norms and framing mechanisms (Risse, 1995; Checkel, 1997; Simmons et al., 2008). Consequently, the Element buttresses the conjecture that the "losers" of the international order can take advantage of international moral claims that spring from strong states and catalyze their positions on global governance.

2 When Do Weak States Win Global Climate Politics Battles and Why?

2.1 National Stakes at International Climate Negotiations

International climate cooperation requires significant domestic adjustments across the world. Strong states that seek to credibly tackle emissions need reforms to internal production and supply chains to lower emissions volumes.

Weak states need more sustainable economic practices as well as adaptation to the disastrous consequences of climate volatility, for they are less self-dependent and more ecologically vulnerable. For both types of countries, meaningful cooperation relies on the domestic political will of adopting climate policy. Along these lines, the literature agrees that the domestic politics of climate change cooperation directly determines countries' position on climate issues and the energy they invest on bargaining over climate agreements (Sprinz & Vaahtoranta, 1994; Ward et al., 2001; Andresen & Agrawala, 2002).

Like studies that turn the attention to the domestic sources of weak states' power in other policy areas (e.g., Katzenstein, 1985; Milner & Kubota, 2005), the scholarship on the domestic drivers of global climate cooperation highlights a number of mechanisms for domestic position-taking and bargaining motivation. These mechanisms seem to generally apply across different types of countries. Some scholars point to the transnational role of industrial lobbies in buttressing climate policy positions (Bernhagen, 2008; Lachapelle & Paterson, 2013; Schulze & Tosun, 2013). Others indicate the influence of domestic civil society organizations on climate cooperation preferences (Betsill & Corell, 2008; Böhmelt, 2013). Similarly, a body of research points to the effect of elections on UNFCCC positions of developed (Rootes, 2008) and developing countries (Hochstetler & Viola, 2012). Overall, this research suggests that domestic economic and political structures similarly matter for weak and strong states' bargaining power. So, in light of the fact that domestic factors may be equally relevant across states and similar mechanisms may drive countries' behavior, some have argued that strong and weak states may have similar tools to ensure that their positions are taken seriously and global agreements are reached (von Stein, 2008).[4]

It is also reasonable to think that strong and weak countries may attain comparable levels of successes at climate negotiations because of the "issue context" – in other words, how the bargaining issues are split across nations (McKibben, 2013). The climate negotiation agenda is famously divided among issues that are more naturally pertinent to industrialized countries and issues that are more focal to less industrialized states. Article 4 of the UNFCCC text asserts that developed (Annex I) nations bear the responsibility for mitigation and technological leadership. The rest of the nations are expected to take action following domestic necessities of adaptation via international incentives, such

---

[4] This can be true even if compliance means different things to strong and weak states (Abbott & Snidal, 2000).

as the Clean Development Mechanism (CDM) or international climate aid programs targeting biodiversity and reforestation. Along these lines, the literature has shown that developed countries have consistently concentrated on issues of mitigation commitments and regulatory instruments (Gupta, 2010). Vice versa, non-developed countries have mostly kept a close focus on issues related to equity principles, such as the responsibility of historical emissions and the opportunities for sustainable development (Michaelowa & Michaelowa, 2015).

In this light, upon the assumption that strong and weak states have high salience on their respective set of issues, one may expect that what is most needed to determine the bargaining outcome on each set of issues is *domestic salience*. In other words, if the conditions exist for strong and weak countries to feel passionately about their most pertinent bargaining points, then this theory suggests that intrinsic salience should push their leaders to appeal to the most crucial domestic interests and direct the way of the negotiations over those issues (Ward et al., 2001; Harrison & Sundstrom, 2007). For example, if a strong country has the ambition to dominate international clean technology markets, its leader may push for more ambitious cooperation terms on that issue. By contrast, if a country faced high costs from enacting an international climate regulation, then the leader may well push against more cooperation.

Evidently, domestic forces may not agree on their country's unitary position on an international climate policy issue. Just like in trade (Milner & Rosendorff, 1996), domestic actors may clash when it comes to international policy goals. In this Element I do not seek to articulate an argument for how domestic actors are internally weighted, nor is the main goal to determine whether one domestic group may be more or less likely to shape national attitudes toward global climate negotiations than another. It is recognized that a range of factors may affect bargaining salience, from private interests (industrial lobbies) to public organizations (civil society groups). The point here is that, as more domestic actors focus and deliberate over a climate policy issue, domestic salience increases. Irrespective of their ideal level of (more or less) cooperation, the urgency attached to an issue signals a stronger commitment for one specific agreement. Hence, this logic suggests that more salience should lead to a more credible position and a higher likelihood of bargaining success (Matthews, 1989).

To be clear, the literature also indicates that other forms of power may be important drivers of weak states' influence. Exploiting institutional procedures and eliciting authority from other formal actors is one noteworthy strategy for bargaining success. Some research indicates that "outlier-like" positions and an orientation toward pivot players can also help weak countries

(Greif et al., 1994). To that end, the most compelling evidence comes from European Union (EU) scholarly research. Bailer's (2004) analysis of policy proposals at the EU Council of Ministers shows that the strategic extremity of positions taken with respect to relevant actors such as the European Commission has important effects on the influence of small countries in shaping EU intergovernmental agreements. Also within the context of the European Union, Bjoerkdahl (2008) indicates the tactical importance of "norm advocacy" by means of attracting the positions of authoritative figures such as the EU Council Secretariat (p. 149). Similarly, Jakobsen (2009) suggests that attempting to be an honest "broker" generated success among small Nordic countries in past EU security negotiations. The importance of strategic positions may be relevant to the climate negotiations too, as some scholars have pointed out (Depledge, 2008). However, weak states at the UNFCCC do not need to rely on institutional formalities as much as in other institutions, given that nation-states are de facto the only actors engaged in the climate negotiations and no other forms of governance have decision-making power on the climate.

The training and intrinsic motivation of individual delegation members are also important alternative explanations of weak states' success. Industrious delegates are likely to be able diplomats and good orators. Preparation matters too: information access and technical training may support a country's capability to persuade other countries of the benefits of its preferred outcomes (Bauer, 2006). Diplomatic competence was certainly impactful in the course of the Kyoto Protocol negotiations. Chasek (2001), for example, claims that in the 1990s the development of agenda points and agreement drafts required a constant reliance on a specific pool of experts. Similarly, Michaelowa and Michaelowa (2012) note that India's elite, "well-versed in the use of the English language, and experienced in the international arena through a high representation in international organization obviously represented a key advantage" (p. 578). These are valuable additional explanations of weak states' influence. However, they also are partly endogenous to preferences: After all, delegates and diplomats would use all their training and motivation if they deemed advocating for an issue a matter of high national interest. In the interest of space, in what follows I therefore stick to a discussion of domestic salience.

2.2 Theories of Salience at International Climate Negotiations

A number of studies of countries' positions on global climate cooperation support the aforementioned claim that salience is linked to international bargaining power. Accordingly, strong countries have more credibility in enhancing uncompromising demands, because they have the capability to unilaterally propose policies that would affect international climate agreements

(Ward, 1996; Okereke et al., 2009). In fact, even the disagreeing studies that highlight the implausibility of unilateral climate action agree on the weight of strong countries' commitments on their most salient UNFCCC issues (Boehringer, 2014). Along these lines, there is evidence that in the early 2000s the executive leaders of strong countries in the European Union settled the international outcomes on carbon capture and emissions trading as electorate concerns put pressure on their action for reduction targets (Schreurs & Tiberghien, 2007; Skovgaard, 2013). Similarly, research on Canada and the United States indicates that domestic waves of public discussions over climate science and the rising value of climate change in political parties' platforms were crucial drivers of the countries' agreed levels of 1990s Kyoto targets (Harrison, 2007).

The salience theory of climate bargaining success would appear to apply to weak countries, too. Accordingly, these should be more successful at influencing the outcomes of their natural UNFCCC issues, for – especially if adequately coordinated and communicated (Majeski & Fricks, 1995) – their commitment on those issues is authoritative, not least because weak states often have a numerical advantage at international organizations (Drahos, 2003). Some scholars have indeed claimed that weak states at the climate negotiations have systematically spent more time discussing the details of capacity-building provisions, knowledge transfer, and adaptation, in order to shape agreements over them (Adger, 2001; Grasso, 2010).

Yet the evidence on whether salience of these states has a direct impact on bargaining success is less clear than for strong states. The empirical research on the topic has found ambiguous effects of salience-based models of success at climate negotiations, especially on issues tilted toward weak states' preferences such as climate finance and the set-up of adaptation programs (Weiler, 2012; Sprinz et al., 2016). The mixed findings do not seem to be related to specific definitions of weak states or specific measurements of bargaining success. Also importantly, the results do not seem to depend on failures of preference aggregation and coordination.

For example, it took until 2018 for loss and damage to be settled as a specific Paris Agreement rule-book point, despite the fact that most developing states had already settled on their terms in 2014. As Prime Minister of Tuvalu Enele Sosene Sopoaga formulated in interviews in 2015:

> *We are all converted and we are all singing one song.* [However,] *the debate so far has been overwhelmed and dominated mainly by technology, business, saving industries, saving economies.*[5]

---

[5] The African, Caribbean and Pacific Group of States. Interview with Prime Minister of Tuvalu. July 20, 2015. www.acp.int/content/acp-interview-special-prime-minister-tuvalu-climate-change. The GroundTruth Project. "Telling of danger at home, island nations gain

Mr Sopoaga mentioned the commitment of the Small Islands to "sing their song louder." At the same time, he made his biggest case around the problem of *vulnerability*:

> *This year in March we had tropical cyclone Pam that hit the islands of the Pacific, particularly Vanuatu, and left a lot of devastation, but also equally in the Solomon Islands, Tuvalu, Kiribati and the Marshall Islands. [...] These [cyclones] are heavily and strongly influenced by climate change. [So] the message that I'm bringing today is one of help. Please save Tuvalu.*[6]

These quotations offer two relevant insights. First, they underline how salience for weak states may be necessary to substantiate a credible position at the climate negotiations but not sufficient. Evidently, the frustration of small islands such as Tuvalu with global inaction on climate change has been detailed since the 1980s (Ashe et al., 1999) yet their salience per se clearly did not generate enough momentum for international climate action until more recently. Second, the quotes above highlight the narrative of climate vulnerability in relation to the relevance weak countries attached to some issues. The exploitation of vulnerability in order to advance specific issues at the UNFCCC is indeed something reported in case studies of the Alliance of Small Island States (AOSIS), the intergovernmental organization of low-lying coastal and small island countries whose main purpose has been to consolidate voices of small island developing countries to address climate change. Research by Betzold (2010), for example, suggests that a remarkable achievement of this organization in the 1990s and early 2000s was to link legitimate perceptions of external vulnerability to mobilized interest for specific agreement terms (for similar arguments, see also Chasek, 2005 and Betzold et al., 2012).

In what follows I concentrate on this intuition and explore its generalizability for countries beyond the AOSIS. In so doing, I elaborate on why salience may empower weak states *only if* coupled with external perceptions of climate vulnerability and discuss how these perceptions motivate strong countries to concede power.

2.3 The Ambivalent Role of Issue Salience for Weak States

Weak states are likely to experience losses from the implementation of global climate policies because of the steep costs of domestic adjustment. The negative costs of emission abatement are higher the more rural and internationally

---

support for 1.5 degree warming target." December 9, 2015. thegroundtruthproject.org/telling-of-danger-at-home-island-nations-gain-support-for-1-5-degree-warming-target

[6] The African, Caribbean and Pacific Group of States. Interview with Prime Minister of Tuvalu. July 20, 2015. www.acp.int/content/acp-interview-special-prime-minister-tuvalu-climate-change.

dependent the states, because these rely on natural resources and tend to lack efficient mitigation technology (Barrett, 2007). Even adaptation policies, which belong to the realm of issues closer to weak states, can entail costly adjustments, for example in the form of investing in protection infrastructure (Forsyth, 2007). At the same time, for these states the high costs of climate cooperation clash with the alternative costs of losing their territory, for example coastal lands and economically precious ecosystems. The price to be paid for climate inaction is essentially their de facto existence.

The way these cost considerations may affect the influence of weak states at international climate negotiations is fundamentally rooted in the broader discussion of weak states' power at international organizations. According to the scholars who see in international organizations an opportunity for small states to protectively promote their attitudes (Abbott & Snidal, 1998; Koremenos et al., 2001; Keohane, 2005), climate negotiations provide the tools to persuasively argue for their preferred international climate policy outcomes. As a result, less powerful states have credible reasons to threaten to stall the negotiations if they think they are doomed anyway. This tactic can be especially effective in a consensus-based voting organization such as the UNFCCC, where states can often exploit fears of negotiation breakdown to link the fate of some issues to bargaining allowances (Schelling, 1960). To that end, stepping out of the talks can lead to international concessions. This is because it is in no state's interest to allow exploitative international agreements, which would force non-legally bound states to refuse to engage in the long run (Schneider, 2011; Urpelainen, 2011b). Consequently, the cost of survival would allow less powerful countries to settle agreements on their more salient issues.

This view is contested by the scholars who see international organizations as constraints on states outside of classical power hierarchies (Axelrod, 1997; Hafner-Burton & Montgomery, 2006). Accordingly, when the rules of bargaining are set up by strong countries, the preoccupations of weak states only deteriorate their position, for strong states know they can manipulate the bargaining agenda in order to maintain absolute power over international policy. At climate negotiations, this view has been supported by those who think weak states have no credibility refusing to bargain, for they are chained to the negotiations at the speed of the laggards (Ward et al., 2001). Similarly, the EU bargaining literature indicates that higher salience implies impatience, which can induce small countries to accept worse deals (Thomson et al., 2006).

These two perspectives clash on how they see the attitude of weak states on their most important issues. In other words, they fundamentally disagree on the role of *salience* for weak states' power in international relations. But while the two takes are often treated and tested in juxtaposition, I argue that they largely coexist, and in fact offset each other. On the one hand, an institution such as the UNFCCC may provide paramount opportunities for weak states to be physically relevant for international regulations. Along these lines, it has been recorded that weak countries at times have threatened to veto the process. For example, in the run-up to Copenhagen, India's leadership stressed that it was unwilling to accept binding mitigation targets for developing countries, echoing issues of injustice against poorer nations (Falkner et al., 2010). On the other hand, it has been made clear that weak states suffer from credibility problems that force their leaders to accept agreements that are suboptimal to their domestic audiences. As historians of international climate politics suggest, opportunities and compromises by weak states have often co-occurred, and are one reason why the current institution is disliked but no alternate institution has yet formed (Underdal, 2017).

This reasoning leads to my consideration that the cost of surviving climate change and the cost of keeping the negotiations alive neutralize each other. These two forces seem to push domestic valence in opposite directions, therefore diluting the power of salience as a credible international commitment device for weak states. Evidently, some subsection of the population at home does care about national liability and "existential threat." The public of weak states may be able to translate this sentiment into loud demonstration at the UNFCCC, and these pushes may provide confidence to weak countries' leaders in representing domestic concerns at international climate meetings. However, this also creates the risk that leaders may come back from the negotiations with nothing. In a world where the bargaining agenda and international resources are in the hands of strong countries, this may leave weak countries' leaders with no alternative but accepting suboptimal agreements (Payne, 2001; Busby, 2016). Consequently, and despite significant efforts to maneuver international climate negotiations toward their preferred outcomes, more vulnerable states may not succeed in international bargaining.

But if salience is not a sufficient condition for success at international climate negotiations for weak states, does it have a role to play for weak states' bargaining power after all? As some research has claimed, weak states have often used vivid displays of climate change–induced disasters to make their case in the course of the UNFCCC meetings. These efforts have increased the visibility of vulnerable countries' negotiation positions and persuaded other parties on some common actions (de Agueda Corneloup & Mol, 2014). Building on this observation, the next section discusses how climate vulnerability not only compels affected countries to push a hard line for the issues they care about *but* is also relevant to the domestic politics of stronger states.

2.4 Eliciting Power from Abroad: Foreign Perceptions of Vulnerability and the Moral Case of Weak States in Strong Countries

In this Element weak states largely overlap with vulnerable states, in that I conceptualize vulnerable nations as weak states with discernible levels of objective urgency to combat climate change. Facing the urgency of climate change requires resources, and vulnerability is in several ways related to a country's level of economic and governance capacity. At the same time, it is not fully endogenous to development and growth, for it is also related to geography and exposure to specific climate-induced natural events. The characteristics that make up the vulnerability profile of a country influence their positions on the issues discussed at the UNFCCC. As I argue here, the sense of objective vulnerability to climate change may in fact embolden these positions.

Vulnerability is a continuum, and weak countries have different levels of vulnerability. Similarly, and independently of their level of climate risk, the salience they attach to their closest issues may also vary. I argue that, *if* climate-vulnerable countries place high levels of salience on issues in their core issue set, they may have the normative legitimacy to pursue them (Harris, 2009). The intuition here is similar to other studies of international relations that observe the impact of physical resilience on bargaining success at international organizations. For example, Simmons and Guzman (2005) suggest that weaker countries at the World Trade Organization tend to choose to bring bigger countries to court, because of limited resources that make them more concentrated on pursuing competitors with larger international weight (larger markets). Likewise, Urpelainen (2011a) implies that weak states are more likely to shame more powerful countries because they have the credibility to claim that large powers are exploiting international system.

Along these lines, I claim that the more climate-vulnerable states are, the more legitimate their concerns. The mechanism I concentrate on, however, is that vulnerability resonates on the *domestic politics of strong states* (Buchanan & Keohane, 2006). Specifically, I maintain that strong countries' reflection of weak countries' climate vulnerability is a necessary condition for the former countries to consent to their positions on their most salient issues. In what follows, I explain how strong countries accept weak countries' salient positions based on a number of expectations about leadership accountability and "audience costs" (Fearon, 1994).

Governments are motivated by the domestic punishment that leaders may incur for misrepresenting, reconsidering, or reversing public wishes about foreign policy. In the context of climate politics, where leaders of strong states are sensitive to punishments for ignoring normative rules of international conduct (Abbott & Snidal, 2000), they may have the legal right to ignore the demands of vulnerable parties but may not do that to avoid the political costs. This behavior may be especially true in democracies where domestic political groups can coordinate to punish leaders for foreign policy stands (Tomz & Weeks, 2013). However, international reputation is valued by autocratic leaders too (Weeks, 2008). Along these lines, developed countries seem willing to avoid diplomatic circumstances that may cause political instability at home, such as voters' resentment against leaders' immoral actions abroad (Simmons, 2000).

Evidently, the public to which strong countries' leaders are accountable may not be receptive to the concerns of weak countries all the time, if at all. That said, there is evidence that people are often attuned to the broad themes discussed at the UNFCCC negotiations, if only because of domestic "pull factors" that focus the attention on the issue by framing the negotiations around the morality of helping countries vulnerable to climate change (Risse et al., 1999; Simmons, 2009). For example, in climate politics NGOs use persuasion and coercion to refocus the attention of the public and of leaders on the paramount challenges of weak states (Prakash & Gugerty, 2010; Allan & Hadden, 2017).

NGOs can threaten consequences for the failure to reach agreement on these high-profile issues. Importantly, they elevate the moral dimensions of the problem, drawing attention to the connection between climate vulnerability, social justice, and international redistribution (Ringius et al., 2002; Rübbelke, 2011). This connection is known to resonate with leaders of strong states. Some studies have shown that, when pushed by moral framing, world leaders show desire to appear virtuous (Busby, 2010). This is plausibly because being reminded of the lawfulness of the international distribution of domestic burdens generates "kind behavior" (Grant & Keohane, 2005; Kertzer & Rathbun, 2015) or, alternately, because ignoring a call for kindness toward more vulnerable countries could cause hurtful shaming (Downs & Jones, 2002). There is also some evidence that moral framing mobilizes other sections of society involved in climate politics, such as business groups, which become more sensitized to campaigns for climate aid in developing countries (Genovese, 2019). All these domestic mechanisms are known to influence the public and, by consequence, the perception that their leaders may have of the importance that domestic voters place on fairness at the UNFCCC. Back to my argument, I hold that the public connection between climate risks and considerations of global justice in strong countries puts leaders on the alert to concede some power to vulnerable states on issues that pertain to their struggles.

This association between global justice, climate change issues, and vulnerable states is evident in media attention around the UNFCCC climate negotiations. One measure of such public attention is the Google Trends data shown in Figure 2.1. The three graphs show the time series of Google searches for words related to "climate risk" and "poor countries" (the closest approximation of weak countries by Google searches) for each week between January 2016 and January 2019, the years for which Google Trends has the highest quality data. The graphs correspond to a world sample, a US sample, and a UK sample; the United States and the United Kingdom were chosen not only because they are well represented in the Google Trends data (they have the highest search volume index) but also because they can be considered two strong states in international politics. Following the theory, the annual climate meetings of the Conference of the Parties (COPs) should increase the attention that the world, and especially strong states, would pay to the connection between climate and vulnerability. Along these lines, the graphs show two interesting patterns. First, the two time series are highly correlated across all three graphs (Pearson r is 0.45, 0.35, and 0.21 for each respective sample). Second, there is a significant increase in searches of the key terms preceding and during the COPs, as indicated by the point biserial correlations.[7]

These patterns are purely illustrative, but they indicate the extent of public reflection generated at the time of the UNFCCC meetings and its possible implications for choices of strong states' leadership at the climate negotiations. But it is important to recall that my theory specifies that the connection between climate vulnerability and the moral case of weak states should be compelling mainly for issues closest to weak states' coordinated interests. This is because of the way issues are naturally set up and linked at the climate negotiations (Victor, 2006). It is also a function of the fact that weak states' issues make the association between climate risks, justice, and weakness vivid, ensuring that no ambiguity is left regarding their need for compensation (Mills, 2005). This connection between climate vulnerability and norms appeals to transnational audiences and makes it particularly hard for strong states' leaders to argue against their most sensitive domestic players (Schreurs & Tiberghien, 2007).[8] Hence, I expect that the increased attention of strong countries' publics

---

[7] The shown trends are analogous if one tracks the words "developing countries" or "vulnerable states" instead of "poor countries," although the latter are more searched in absolute terms and provide better illustrations.

[8] Conceding on those issues is also a more efficient strategy for strong countries if they want to retain vetoing power on mitigation issues. If weak countries stand to lose from a policy issue, delaying cooperation on such issue may be the dominant strategy, because it may convince strong states to accommodate and provide rents (Leebron, 2002; Simmons & Guzman, 2005; Lyne et al., 2006).

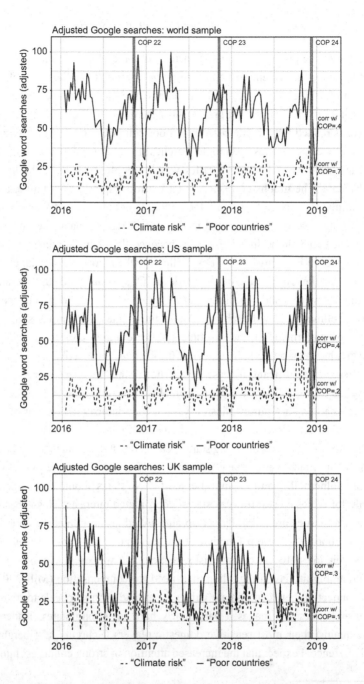

Figure 2.1 Weak states and climate risk in the international public imaginary

Notes: The graphs show Google Trends data for adjusted searches of the phrases "climate risk" and "poor countries" for samples of world, US, and UK citizens, respectively. The red bars indicate the weeks in which a climate negotiation round (a COP) has occurred. The point biserial correlations between each search series and the COP dummy are reported in the graphs. The correlations between the two series are 0.45, 0.35, and 0.21 for each respective sample (from top to bottom).

to climate change vulnerability and the additional legitimacy this gives to the salience of weak states only work so far at making strong countries' leaders give concessions on a subset of UNFCCC issues set up for developing countries.

An illustration of this phenomenon is delineated for two distinct climate bargaining issues in Figure 2.2. Figure 2.2 refers to news produced in the course of the annual COPs between 2008 and 2014, which reflect some of the most central years discussed in this Element. The data source is *LexisNexis*, a stable and reliable (English) news source database. The data are based on all available news media articles that include the words "climate," "risk" and (alternately) "development assistance" or "reduction targets." Development assistance and reduction targets are both prominent issues discussed at COPs throughout history. Importantly, weak states prioritize "development assistance" in relation to adaptation (Gupta, 2010), while "reduction targets" are more critical to the developed nations legally bound to emissions reductions (at least at the time under consideration).

The top panel clearly shows reduction targets are a significantly more prominent issue of the UNFCCC negotiations as reported in Anglophone news. The absolute number of news containing "development assistance" observed between 2008 and 2014 is 394, while for "reduction targets" it is 1,839. But, importantly, the connection with climate risk is more accentuated with respect to the former issue, which is clearly more linked to development and vulnerability (bottom panel). On average across the observed years, 30 percent of the "development assistance" news mentioned "climate risk" with respect to 20 percent of the "reduction targets" news, suggesting that the issue of development assistance was systematically tied to vulnerability, at least according to the media reporters. While these patterns remain unpacked, they suggest that the framing of the issues most dear to weak states at the negotiations is strongly connected to perceptions of climate risk and vulnerability. This framing, I argue, generates the moral legitimacy of weak countries' climate policy requests and pushes strong countries' leaders to concede agreements.

The rest of the Element seeks to test this theory by analyzing country preferences and bargaining positions at historical climate negotiations. The central hypothesis is that, conditional on a certain salience on a relevant issue, weak states should be more likely to decide the outcome of the negotiation on that issue as their vulnerability to climate change increases. This expectation has a number of empirical implications. First, it suggests that the amount of salience attached to an issue may matter only for certain countries, presumably the most powerful countries, for salience is not enough of a credibility device for less resilient and more globally dependent nations. Second, vulnerability may be especially compelling for weak states' issues in case they are ready to battle

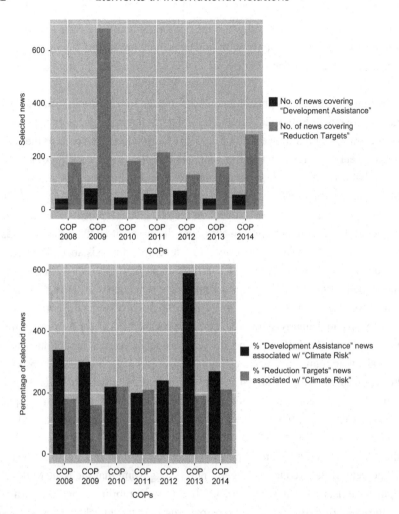

Figure 2.2 Climate risk and weak states' climate negotiations issues in the international press

Notes: The bar plot shows the percentages of news media articles found in *Lex-isNexis* that include the words "climate," "risk" and (alternately) "development assistance" -or- "reduction targets," both issues that were highly prominent in discussions at COPs throughout history. The percentages are calculated in relation to the number of news media articles mentioning "climate" and "development assistance" and "reduction targets" only (without risk). The data are based on articles that were published within the two weeks of each COP between 2008 and 2014. It is based on English media only and excluded documents with fewer than 500 words.

and to have a less compelling role for strong states, which are inherently less vulnerable but also do not possess the same "allies" the weak states have, such as NGOs and other transnational climate advocates (including clean energy companies).

Before introducing the data to test the claims delineated thus far, a couple of caveats are worth mentioning. First, my theory relies on the assumption that national positions can be compared in systematic ways. While all observational measurements of positions at international negotiations are necessarily limited, I argue that national positions at climate negotiations can be investigated in a "spatial" fashion. Consequently, I hold that spatial models of bargaining can be helpful in testing the "weight" that weak states' characteristics have on outcome attainment at the UNFCCC. This is not new to the study of international bargaining preferences in international relations, but it is to international climate negotiation studies (see Sprinz et al., 2016, for a notable exception).

Additionally, I assume it is possible to identify which UNFCCC issues belong to the core issue set of strong and weak states, respectively. There is a large literature on how climate policy issues are historically introduced on the UNFCCC agenda. This literature makes clear, for example, that the "polluter-pays" principle and the concept of "historical but differentiated responsibility" are most evident in the speeches of poor countries (Jinnah, 2017). Similarly, the issue of adaptation finance is most associated with Least Developed Countries (LDC), which at the CoPs in Marrakech (2001) mobilized international nongovernmental actors in order to legitimize the need for a global adaptation fund (Kasa et al., 2008). This is not to say that weak states do not care about strong states' positions on their core issues, or vice versa. Rather, it is to say that there may be clustering of issues based on the character of the issue, and that such clustering can be extrapolated from the data, as I show in the following sections.

3 Measuring Preferences and Success at Global Climate Change Conferences

To evaluate the central argument of the Element, I resort to a number of original measurements of national preferences, negotiation outcomes, and subsequent measures of bargaining success. The data collection relied on a dictionary-based text analysis that yielded estimates of agreements, disagreements, countries' ideal positions, and saliences for a large number of issues at the climate negotiations. The final dataset covers 115 countries at two negotiation periods, namely the pre-Kyoto Protocol enforcement negotiations (2001–2004) and the post-Kyoto Protocol negotiations (2008–2012). In what follows I describe the data sources and structure, and introduce the variables used in the main empirical analysis.

3.1 UNFCCC Negotiations Data: Positions, Salience, and Outcomes

The UNFCCC negotiations dataset presented here was originally collected to overcome two limitations with the empirical climate negotiations literature: the absence of spatial measurements of UNFCCC negotiations and the scarcity of "large" comparative data across countries involved at these meetings. In order to fill these gaps and provide a broader delineation of climate change bargaining, my data seek to extract UNFCCC bargaining parameters of single nations and their collective aggregation from observational sources, namely official UNFCCC texts (Genovese, 2014).

For the country-specific bargaining variables (i.e., issue-specific *national positions* and *salience*), the data collection concentrated on the UNFCCC National Communications, which each UNFCCC member state submits to the COP every four years in order to meet commitments under the Convention.[9] For the aggregate bargaining variables (i.e., collective *agreements* and *disagreements*), I focused on the decision-making texts produced at the end of the official meetings of the 2001/2004 and 2008/2011 COPs, respectively. The data collection focused on issues at two separate times of the climate negotiations: the pre-Kyoto Protocol ratification years (2001–2004) and the post-Kyoto Protocol negotiations (2008–2011), which constituted important bargaining moments at the international climate meetings.[10]

In terms of issues under investigation, I relied on a combination of approaches in order to identify the most controversial agenda points discussed at the UNFCCC COPs in the years under analysis. Specifically, I identified the bargaining issues by cross-validating the negotiation summaries of the reporting service "Earth Negotiation Bulletin" as well as articles available online. Additionally, I used a deductive approach to verify these issues using key words from secondary sources and newspapers.[11] The issue identification exercise points to twenty-two issues for the first bargaining period (2001–2004) and twenty-three for the second bargaining period (2008–2011), which I list in Table 3.1. As indicated, issues like the *differentiated responsibility* principle

---

[9] Not all countries submit these documents at the required times. Sometimes countries submitted a communication only at one point in time. While this generates some issues of selection, for the time under consideration there are only few cases of countries that submitted no communication at all.

[10] Moreover, these two periods correspond to sets of years when countries submitted National Communications to the UNFCCC, thus providing elicited preferences for issues discussed around the same time of these negotiations. The premises of the data collection are described in detail in Genovese (2014).

[11] Genovese (2014) describes the parameters chosen to judge which issues were more significantly debated and thus which issues were eventually excluded.

Table 3.1 Bargaining issues at UNFCCC, 2001–2011

Period 1		Period 2	
Issue	**Scale**	**Issue**	**Scale**
1. CDM engagement	Ordinal	1. CDM engagement	Ordinal
2. Emission trading	Ordinal	2. Emission trading	Ordinal
3. Binding commitment	Ordinal	3. Binding commitment	Ordinal
4. LUCF accounting	Ordinal	4. LUCF historical records	Ordinal
5. Funding approach	Ordinal	5. Funding approach	Ordinal
6. Abatement credits	Ordinal	6. Abatement credits	Ordinal
7. LUCF eligible threshold	Ordinal	7. REDD eligible threshold	Ordinal
8. Nuclear energy use	Ordinal	8. Nuclear energy use	Ordinal
9. Technological transfers	Ordinal	9. CCS adoption	Ordinal
10. Adaptation support	Continuous	10. Adaptation support	Continuous
11. LUCF-based abatement	Continuous	11. Technological transfers	Continuous
12. GHG abatement target	Continuous	12. GHG abatement target	Continuous
13. Int'l accountability	Continuous	13. Int'l accountability	Continuous
14. Legislative action level	Continuous	14. Legislative action level	Continuous
15. Offset projects credit	Continuous	15. Offset projects credit	Continuous
16. Regulatory approach	Continuous	16. Regulatory approach	Continuous
17. Systematic observation	Continuous	17. Systematic observation	Continuous

Table 3.1 *(continued)*

Period 1		Period 2	
Issue	**Scale**	**Issue**	**Scale**
18. Historical responsibility	Binary	18. ODA diversion	Ordinal
19. Supplementarity	Binary	19. Post-2012 regime	Ordinal
20. ODA diversion	Binary	20. Temperature rise limit	Ordinal
21. Proportional industry impact	Binary	21. Int'l bunkers	Ordinal
22. Uncertainty of policy	Binary	22. Historical responsibility	Binary
		23. Supplementarity	Binary

Notes: The table reports the issues included in the dataset for which countries' positions and bargaining outcomes are measured. Period 1 corresponds to the UNFCCC negotiations between 2001 and 2004 and is associated to the bargaining of the Marrakesh Agreement (2004). Period 2 corresponds to the negotiations between 2008 and 2011 and is associated to the bargaining of the Durban Agreement (2011). Acronyms: CDM: Clean Development Mechanism; LUCF: Land Use Change and Forestry; REDD: Reduction of Emissions from Deforestation and Forest Degradation; CCS: Carbon Capture and Storage. Note that the binary issues are excluded from the analysis in the paper as the NBS model automatically defaults into the least cooperative outcome, that is, the status quo (0) outcome.

are discussed throughout the whole series of two periods in the dataset. Others like *carbon capture and storage* emerged at only one of the two observed periods. Based on the denotation of the debates in the UNFCCC texts and the Earth Negotiation Bulletin sources, some of the issues are defined as continuous (e.g., the percentage of emissions each country plans to cut with reforestation), while others are best measured as ordinal or binary.

Following the applied bargaining literature on international organizations (e.g., Mansfield et al., 2000; Thomson et al., 2006), I then gathered bargaining information in a spatial fashion – meaning that, for each identified issue debated at the UNFCCC, I situated country and aggregate parameters on a unidimensional spectrum resembling Figure 3.1. Accordingly, the negotiation agreement O is one point in a continuum of possible outcomes, which is determined by the distance between the status quo, d, and the ideal position x of country i over issue j. I now describe in detail how I collected the issue-specific agreement

Figure 3.1 Spatial illustration of the bargaining measurements

Notes: This figure sketches how each bargaining parameter was measured for the purposes of data collection. Each data point is measured in a linear space for each issue j where d is the disagreement point, O is the outcome, and x is the elicited bargaining preference (i.e., the ideal national position) for all the countries.

and disagreement points and, for each country, the issue-specific positions and salience.

3.1.1 Collective Bargaining Parameters: Status Quo and Negotiation Outcomes

In concordance with the international bargaining literature, *disagreement* point (d) is conceptualized as the minimum possible level of cooperation. Practically, this corresponds to the starting point of each negotiations, which is the agreement from the preceding negotiations. In my dataset, the decision texts ruling at the beginning of the observed UNFCCC periods are used to measure these "disagreement" points. They are the decision texts of the Bonn conference in 2001 (COP06) and of the Poznan negotiations in 2008 (COP14). Numerically, the disagreement parameters are assigned a value of zero across all issues, to represent a consistent status quo. By contrast, *agreement* points (O) correspond to the decisions in the texts at the end of the bargaining periods. Specifically, the agreements for period 1 correspond to the decisions made in Buenos Aires in 2004 (COP10), while the agreements for period 2 correspond to the decisions made in Durban in 2011 (COP17).

Quantifying the outcome points required a careful assessment of the agreement texts as well as an evaluation of how these relate to the disagreement points. Practically speaking, I measured the issue-specific outcomes by first scaling each issue according to the conflict reported in the secondary sources (e.g the Earth Negotiation Bulletin). Then, based on a qualitative content analysis of the decision texts, I assigned the value that matches the spatial point where the outcome was settled. The result is a distribution of outcomes across the 45 identified issues. The agreements show substantive variation, especially for the first bargaining period. This is consistent with the historical accounts that describe the "Copenhagen negotiation era" as a particularly tight bargaining time (Dimitrov, 2010). Nevertheless, there is noteworthy variation in the outcomes of the second bargaining period as well.[12]

---

[12] More information on the outcome estimates is reported in the Appendix.

3.1.2 National Positions and Salience

For the country-level negotiation measurements, I performed a systematized content analysis of the National Communications (NC) that each member country submitted to the COP up to December 2011. Of the 192 UNFCCC member countries, 115 individual countries submitted NCs in at least one of these time periods; 89 submitted their NCs in the years preceding the Kyoto Protocol enforcement, while 84 submitted their next NC in the post–Kyoto Protocol negotiations period. These two groups of countries constitute the sample of states observed in the dataset.[13]

To measure states' *positions*, I divided the NCs into "natural sentences" (i.e., sentences that follow standard grammatical rules) and coded each by assigning it to each applicable issue. I then assigned to each sentence the value that corresponds to the position that the sentence conveyed.[14] Each position can take any value in the spectrum where I identified the agreement points for each issue in Table 3.1. Roughy 15 percent of the position data is missing at random, and I relied on probabilistic imputations for predicting these values.[15]

As a way of clarifying the measurement of the national positions, consider Figure 3.2, which illustrates the coding on the unidimensional bargaining space of the issue whether and how nuclear energy should be used for mitigation purposes. The issue is defined as a four-scale ordinal variable (note that for the analysis I standardize the values so that each issue ranges between zero and one). The lowest value corresponds to the disagreement point and is assigned to countries whose position is farthest to the desire of harmonized multilateral criteria for the use of nuclear energy for mitigation. By contrast, the highest value is assigned to countries that want higher levels of cooperation, intended as regulatory harmonization or integration/legal standardization. Each country's position is identified in either of the points of this spectrum, as well as

---

[13] The list of sampled countries is illustrated in Figure A.2 in the Appendix. In 2001–2004, the observed NCs correspond to NC3 for Annex I and NC1 for Non-Annex I. For 2008–2011, they correspond to NC5 for Annex I and NC2 for Non-Annex I. In their NCs, countries report "emissions and removals of greenhouse gases and details of the activities a Party undertakes to implement the Convention" (UNFCCC, 2012). Moreover, they "contain information on national circumstances, vulnerability assessment, financial resources, and transfer of technology" (UNFCCC, 2012). Consequently, NCs are anchored to the preferences that underline national positions at the UNFCCC meetings and are bound to topics debated at the COP.

[14] This coding is equivalent to the categorization of "quasi sentences" in the Comparative Manifesto Project (Budge et al., 2001). As in this project, issues are assumed to be mutually exclusive, so that the same unit of text cannot be assigned to more than one issue. Certain stages of the data coding employed two coders, and the reliability of the coding is overall acceptable, as discussed in Genovese (2014).

[15] The distribution of selected issues is in Figure A.3 in the Appendix.

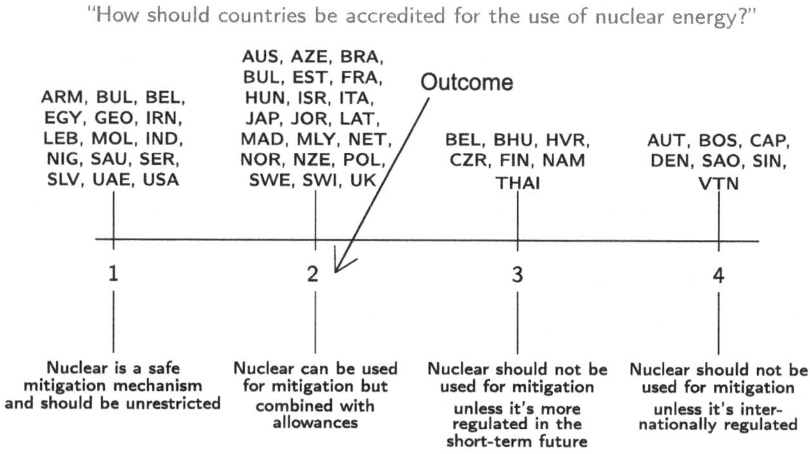

"How should countries be accredited for the use of nuclear energy?"

Figure 3.2 National positions and outcome: A specific issue illustration

Notes: This figure illustrates countries' ideal positions and bargaining outcome on the issue of accounting for mitigation from nuclear energy discussed in 2008–2011.

the final outcome. Notably, some countries happen to be closer to the final outcome. While this may be a function of luck for some states, I argue that in the aggregate it is an indication of influence – something I come back to in the analyses below.

States, however, do not compete only on the premise of their positions. Countries also do so by emphasizing specific issues because, as highlighted earlier in this Element, they place efforts in choosing on which issues to place more *salience*. Consequently, I also measure the salience each state attaches to each agenda issue. The salience indicator here is a byproduct of the coding of positions, as both salience and preferences are assumed to come from a similar data generation process. Specifically, I summed each NC's coded text units per issue, and then calculated the rate of coverage (percent of counts) for each issue a country addresses (Lowe et al., 2011). The final values are measured as percentages of text covered by each issue in each NC.

The summary statistics of the salience measure suggest a sensible amount of variation. The distributions indicate that, although most developing countries tend to emphasize most issues, they do not do it uniformly nor equally. For example, Tanzania and Uruguay address the multilateral funding for mitigation issue for 15 percent of their NCs, which is almost as many times as the United States, while the Democratic Republic of Congo does not address it once. The salience measure is also interesting in light of the theory advanced in this Element. Generally speaking, developed democracies place high salience on their core issues related to mitigation, such as emission trading, reduction targets and binding commitments, while poorer countries place more salience on issues, for example, of use of land use and forestry and official development assistance (ODA). However, there is substantive variation in the way small nations, for example, may emphasize those issues. Consequently, it is not obvious whether salience is relevant after all, at least for less powerful countries. Furthermore, only for some issues positions are highly correlated with salience. These patterns suggest that salience may have different meaningfulness for different countries, as I test later in the analyses.[16]

3.2 Vulnerability

The data described thus far refers to bargaining measurements as observed at the negotiations. However, the crux of my argument is that neither bargaining positions nor issue salience are sufficient to explain the success that marginal states have at climate negotiations – not even on the issues that most naturally refer to their priorities and needs. I have argued that objective climate urgency – as in, climate vulnerability – combined to salience may provide the necessary legitimacy for weak states to be accommodated at the climate negotiations. Here I describe how I measure climate vulnerability.

Several metrics of vulnerability have been developed across the years. The most popular ones range from agricultural and soil resilience (Ahmed et al., 2009) to economic risk of climate change (Hsiang et al., 2017) to energy vulnerability (Carley et al., 2018). Most metrics, however, are country specific, and do not lend themselves to the comparative analysis sought in this Element. Given that my data spread on two different time periods for multiple countries, I here rely on the *Climate Risk Index* (CRI), a comprehensive time-varying measure of countries' vulnerability to the consequences of climate change (Germanwatch, 2019).

CRI is a weighted indicators of deaths and income losses to weather-related loss events (e.g., storms, floods, and heat waves) for each country in the world. It has been released annually since 2005, but presents some ex post measures back until 1995. In order to construct the CRI values for my study, I use the CRI scores averaged for 2000–2004 for the first period of my analysis, and then the CRI scores averaged for 2004–2011 for the second period of my analysis. Figure 3.3 shows the global distribution of more recent CRI scores on a standardized scale from 0 to 100. There is large variation across countries, as

---

[16] Figure A.4 in the Appendix shows the salience scores on selected issues.

Climate Risk Index 2011

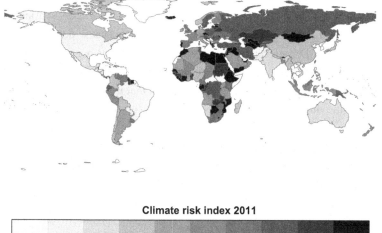

Climate risk index 2011

0   100

Figure 3.3 Climate risk index – global distribution

Sources: This figure shows the distribution of the Climate Risk Index (CRI) for the entire world in 2011. Original values range between 3 and 120 for 2011, and 3 and 175 for the whole range of years aggregated by the analysis presented in the following paragraph.

one would expect. Importantly, the map also indicates that the most climate vulnerable nations are in developing parts of the world. However, some developed countries (e.g., in Europe) also seem at relatively high risk. This could possibly increase the sensibility that some of the domestic actors in developed countries may have to the vulnerability of weaker countries, as argued in this Element.

One caveat, however, is that CRI is heavily dependent on geographical characteristics. Whilst this warrants from issues of endogeneity with national income and policy capacity, CRI scores may overstate structural reasons for climate resilience. Consequently, my analyses also rely on alternative measures to gauge the effect of other aspects of climate vulnerability. For robustness tests, I operationalize the World Bank's Official Development Assistance (ODA) (World Bank, 2012). ODA captures the level of development capacity of a country, and is known to be of relevant consideration when countries discuss capability to mitigate and adopt to climate change (Dutschke & Michaelowa, 2006). Along these lines, some research has even shown a close connection between physical vulnerability to climate change and aid receipt (Betzold

& Weiler, 2018). Empirically, the ODA variable consists of the net level of economic concessions in USD received for development, including pollution abatement projects.[17] It should be clear that compared to the CRI variable the ODA measure is more indirect. It is also less refined, because developed countries have an ODA of zero.[18] Nevertheless, comparing results with the net level of ODA may still be informative because aid receptivity reflects financial constraints that proxy weak states' capabilities, that is, "weakness."[19]

Before moving to investigate how vulnerability correlates with the UNFCCC bargaining data, it is worth making a note on the bivariate relation between the vulnerability indicators and the measures of states' positions and salience discussed earlier. On average across all issues in my dataset, there is no linear relationship between CRI scores and national positions, meaning that more vulnerable countries are not consistently more interested in pushing for ambitious positions on climate cooperation. This seems sensible if one believes in the fundamental difference between strong and weak countries' issues, as delineated in this Element. Accordingly, low and high levels of vulnerability may fail to influence bargaining outcomes *on the aggregate*, but the very vulnerable may ultimately determine the agreements on certain specific issues they place most salience on. Interestingly, correlations between salience and climate risk by issue indicate that on some agenda points originally put forward for developing countries - for example, Land use, land-use change and forestry (LULUCF) targets, ODA conditionality, and systematic monitoring of emissions, the correlation is positive and statistically meaningful.[20] This suggests the important connection between salience and vulnerability argued in my theory and investigated in the following section.

4 Empirical Evidence from Global Climate Negotiations

This section presents the empirical tests of the theory delineated earlier in the Element. First, I discuss the climate negotiation themes under analysis, and

---

[17] ODA includes grants by official agencies of the members of the Development Assistance Committee (DAC), multilateral institutions, and non-DAC countries, minus foreign direct disbursements of aid.

[18] For computational purposes, I assign a 0.001 value to the ODA of all Organization for Economic Cooperation and Development (OECD) countries.

[19] For another additional test, I explored the *Environmental Performance Index* (EPI) developed by the Yale Center for Environmental Law & Policy. This indicator essentially evaluates environmental sustainability, therefore generating a score based on how well countries are addressing environmental vulnerability at home. The scores are constructed through the aggregation of more than twenty indicators reflecting national-level environmental data that include air quality, trend in carbon intensity, biomass protection, and water waste. The results provide some interesting nuance to my central findings, but essentially confirm the main patterns.

[20] See Table A.1 in the Appendix.

reflect on which exact issues one would expect weak states to have more legitimacy as a function of vulnerability. Second, I present an aggregate analysis of bargaining success at the UNFCCC, and an issue-by-issue analysis. Finally, I offer some evidence of the mechanisms within the domestic context of strong states that, according to my theory, drive the aggregate results.

4.1 Issue Clustering: Identifying Strong and Weak States' Issues

A crucial assumption in the international climate negotiations literature is that the bargaining agenda is roughly split among issues closer – on average – to the problems of developed countries and issues more directly involving the problems of less developed countries. I follow this assumption, and rely on the idea that some issues are intrinsically more dominated by the preferences of some countries. This implies that there are different ways in which issues are interpreted and bargained upon, consistent to which type of countries they belong to.

Qualitatively, the literature provides some suggestions for which type of country naturally "possess" which type of issue. For example, some works point to *historical responsibilities* and *adaptation finance* as areas where "the norms [of developing countries] guide the solution" (Gupta, 2012, p. 634). Similarly, arrangements on *land management and use of forests* as carbon sinks are said to be "hostage" to debates of equity, because they systematically require the legitimization of small, agricultural countries (Dimitrov, 2005). At the same time, mitigation-oriented issues at the UNFCCC are often said to be dictated by the legally bound Annex I countries (Bodansky, 2010). This case-specific information provides some initial priors for which issues listed in Table 3.1, one could expect weak states to have more "moral legitimacy." However, an inductive evaluation of the position data can provide further data-driven understanding of which issues may be "closer" to the agenda of the strong states (i.e., the original UNFCCC agenda setters) and which may be outside of their core issues. So, to map the main latent clustering underlying the coded issues, I run a data reduction technique, namely a factor analysis, on the position data.[21]

The factor analysis of the national positions calculates two main latent variables as the main measurements of variation. The loadings on the issues and their respective correlations are particularly interesting. I plot those in the two-dimensional space by bargaining period in Figure 4.1. The issues for which

---

[21] I run the analysis on the dataset with and without the binary issues. I do so because factor analysis requires more complicated assumptions to calculate latent measures with dichotomous variables. Furthermore, as I discuss below, most bargaining models systematically predict a default on the status quo when bargaining positions are ranged on a binary scale. The results presented below refer to a factor analysis that excludes the binary issues.

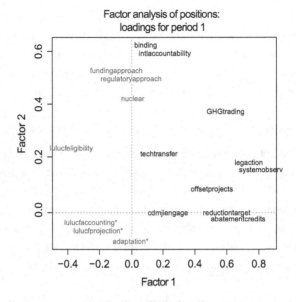

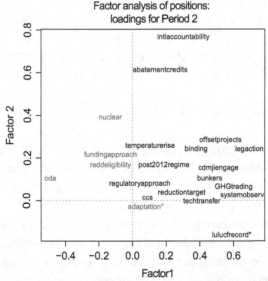

Figure 4.1 Dimensions and divisions across UNFCCC issues

Notes: This figure shows the distribution of the issue-specific national positions within a two-dimension space expressed by the two main principal components. Positions over issues in black represent the main cluster of issues that load prominently on the first estimated factor (right of Factor 1 axis). Positions over issues in gray represent another cluster that fails to load on the first factor. Issues with an asterisk (*) denote positions that in separate, three-factor analyses load on a third estimated principal component.

loadings are positive on both dimensions are placed in the top-right corner of each respective plot (in black). These issues cluster together in what could be interpreted as developed world's climate issues, for example, the type of international *binding treaty* expected after 2012, the level of *reduction targets* to meet, and the terms of *emissions trading*. By contrast, a number of issues cluster outside of the boundaries of these two factors. Specifically, 12 issues are not in the top-right corner covered by the two main latent dimensions. These include issues of *reforestation and deforestation* (e.g., the eligibility of Land Use Change and Forestry), the approach to *multilateral funding*, and the support for *adaptation finance*. These are topics that the literature not only considers salient to developing countries but also associates to issues dominated by equity and global justice claims, that is, arguments that – following my theory – domestic actors in strong states would use to keep their leaders morally accountable to global climate action.[22] For example, issues of deforestation were heavily dominated by a rhetoric around indigenous rights and native communities, which resonated with a number of developed countries' first nations (Schroeder, 2010). Similarly, in the post-Kyoto negotiations adaptation funds were unlocked by rich states when "particular vulnerable" countries justified their necessity (Remling & Persson, 2014).

In light of these considerations, I expect that the mechanism envisioned in this Element is most predominantly in action for the latter set of issues. In other words, I predict that vulnerability, combined with some level of salience, would especially boost bargaining success for weak countries on the issues that are more dispersed and, according to Figure 4.1, loading outside the main estimated factors. In what follows, I test this expectation directly in a regression analysis framework.

4.2 Macro-Analysis: Weak States' Influence at the UNFCCC

4.2.1 Bargaining Success over Strong and Weak States' Issues

I first evaluate my main hypothesis with an analysis of bargaining success across countries at the UNFCCC. "Success," that is, the central outcome variable of this part of the study, is intended as the ability of a country to shape decisions around its ideal policy outcomes (Ward et al., 2001). In line with the spatial literature of bargaining, I employ a spatial metric of success that relates to my measurement of national positions and their distance to the observed final agreements. Drawing on Arregui & Thomson (2009), I use the following equation to construct the dependent variable:

---

[22] See Brown and Corbera (2003) and Grasso (2010) for equity questions around forestry management and adaptation funds.

$$Bargaining\ Success_{ij} = 1 - \left(\frac{|x_{ij} - O_j|}{max_j} \right)$$

where the success of country i on issue j is a function of the absolute distance between that country's position x and the collective outcome O of issue j minimized by the maximal distance each country can have from the outcome O on issue j. One advantage of this metric is that it creates standardized values from 0 (absolute lack of success) to 100 (absolute success). This is by definition an issue-specific variable, and UNFCCC issues may in fact be bundled. Nonetheless, I analyze these positions with hierarchical models, which help evaluate this type of partially clustered measurements.

Figure 4.2 shows the distribution of *Bargaining Success* for two issues for the first bargaining period under analysis (2001–2004). The issue of LULUCF offset eligibility criteria is an issue that is allegedly "owned" by weak countries. Vice versa, strong states are presumably more entitled to decide over the terms of a post-2012 binding treaty. As the bar plots suggest, for each issue the success rate varies meaningfully across countries, with a substantive number finding themselves considerably far away to the final outcome. Importantly, some very vulnerable states attained significant success over the land use issue, while the only states that seem to have significantly influenced the decision over binding terms are some members of the so-called "Umbrella Group" (a coalition of Annex I parties including New Zealand, Canada, and the United States). This anecdotal evidence is generally in line with the contours of my expectations.

In terms of regression, I estimate the following multilevel linear model:

$$Bargaining\ Success_{ij} = \gamma_{00} + \gamma_{01}X_{ij} + \gamma_{02}Issue\ Salience_{ij} + \gamma_{10}Z_i$$

$$+\gamma_{20}Climate\ Risk_i + \gamma_{22}Issue\ Salience_{ij} \times Climate\ Risk_i + \epsilon_{ij} + \delta_{0j} \quad (4.1)$$

in which the issue-level intercepts are given by

$$\beta_{0j} = \gamma_{00} + \gamma_{02}Issue\ Salience_{ij} + \delta_{0j}$$

In the above equations, i refers to countries and j refers to issues. The model assumes that countries "nest" within each UNFCCC issue. In other words, the intercepts of success are allowed to vary across issues. Furthermore, I add a random slope for issue salience, which I expect to explain much of the intercept variance. Following the notation in equation (4.1), γ_{00} is the "grand" mean across countries and issues. The error term ϵ_{ij} indicates how a country's attained success deviates from the mean on each issue, and the error term δ_{0j} shows how the mean success over one specific issue deviates from the grand mean.

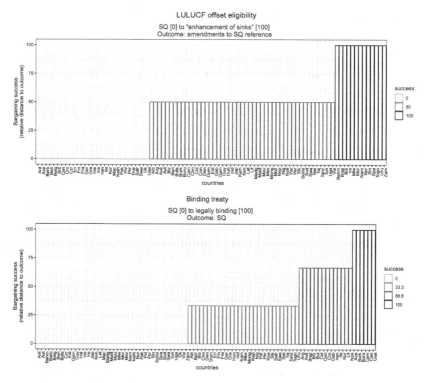

Figure 4.2 Bargaining success LULUCF an illustration across UNFCCC issues

Notes: This figure shows my measure of bargaining success as a distance to the bargaining outcome for two separate issues discussed in Period 1 (COPs between 2001 and 2004). The legend on the right describes the scale of each respective issue. The scale from 0 to 100 denotes the value of "success" for the countries reported at the bottom of the plots.

At the issue-level of analysis, the central variable is *Issue Salience*, ranging from 0 to 1. Generally, I expect this to have a positive sign. But following my theoretical argument, I expect this to be most important at predicting success of strong states, especially on their natural issues. Given the observational set up of the analysis, I also control for alternate issue-level heterogeneity with the variables X. Specifically, I control for *Position Extremity*, which is the standardized distance of each country's issue-specific position to the mean position value in each respective issue space (Schneider, 2009; McKibben, 2013).[23] I also introduce the variable *Issue Complexity*, which is the raw number of long segments coded for each issue (Franchino, 2000).

---

[23] Here I use the mean of all countries' positions, but the median is very similar, correlating at $r = 0.96$ and 0.87 for the two periods.

At the country-level of analysis, the most relevant variable is the *Climate Risk* indicator, which I also standardize on a scale from 0 to 1. I expect climate risks to create a morally compelling case in favor of weak states on their natural issues, granted these put some stakes on them. In line with this reasoning, I interact *Climate Risk* with *Issue Salience*, and I expect this interaction to be positively associated with success, especially on weak states' issues. Finally, in line with conventional practice, I also control for the vector Z of country-level variables. Success at climate negotiations may be a function of features such as income and pollution capacity, and I employ these measures as collected from the World Bank. *GDP per capita* corresponds to the log of the per capita gross domestic product for the years between 2001 and 2004 (Period 1) and 2008 and 2011 (period 2), respectively. *CO2* corresponds to the analogous log of the carbon emission stocks. Finally, I add a period dummy to control for time effects.[24]

Table 4.1 shows the main findings – first, for all the countries on all issues, and then for two different issue subsets. Overall, the estimations indicate that the variance component across all models is statistically significant, and that the difference across issues account for variation in the intercepts of bargaining success. In other words, the multilevel specification seems warranted, as the statistics indicate significantly different patterns across the bargaining issues. Regarding the more substantive results, Model 1 reports the estimates of an unconditional specification across all issues. I find that salience is on average a strong and substantive predictor of bargaining success, overall in line with previous studies (Weiler, 2012). Model 2 instead reports the results with the interaction variable, *Issue salience × Climate risk*. This is also positive and statistically significant, to indicate that as vulnerability increases salience is more associated with bargaining success. Together, the results from these two models suggest that salience is a critical condition for bargaining power, but that it may be especially so if one takes into account the preferences of vulnerable countries, as predicted by my theory. However, these findings do not clarify which sets of issues may be driving the predicting power of salience and the interaction with vulnerability. To explore this, I run subgroup analyses by separating strong states' and weak states' issues, following the division offered by my factor analysis (Figure 4.1).

Models 3 and 4 show the results for the subset of issues that clustered on the dominant latent dimensions, that is, the issues of mitigation standards, and binding targets that the literature usually associates to developed countries. I

---

[24] I use robust (Huber-White) standard errors to allow the within-issue correlation across countries to be anything at all. In the main results do not report the covariance, because its estimate turns into a corner solution (-1) once I include the cross-level interaction.

Table 4.1 Bargaining success across issues at the UNFCCC

	Y: Issue-specific bargaining success					
	All issues		Strong states' issues (Dominant factor loading)		Weak states' issues (Non-dominant factor loading)	
	(1)	(2)	(3)	(4)	(5)	(6)
Issue salience	0.40** (0.16)	−0.16 (0.28)	0.58*** (0.098)	0.012 (0.32)	0.18 (0.36)	−0.48 (0.65)
Climate risk	0.005 (0.014)	−0.029 (0.022)	0.005 (0.019)	−0.034 (0.036)	0.004 (0.025)	−0.028 (0.023)
Issue salience × Climate risk		0.007** (0.003)		0.007 (0.005)		0.008* (0.004)
GDP per capita (ln)	−1.14 (0.87)	−1.14 (0.88)	−1.95* (1.11)	−1.99* (1.14)	0.60 (0.88)	0.64 (0.86)
CO_2 (ln)	0.44 (0.65)	0.44 (0.66)	1.20 (0.75)	1.21 (0.76)	−1.25 (1.00)	−1.27 (0.99)
Position extremity	−0.95** (0.48)	−0.96** (0.48)	−1.08 (0.83)	−1.11 (0.84)	−0.78 (0.58)	−0.76 (0.57)
Issue complexity	−0.004 (0.006)	−0.004 (0.006)	−0.009 (0.009)	−0.010 (0.009)	0.002 (0.002)	0.004 (0.002)

Table 4.1 (continued)

Y: Issue-specific bargaining success

	All issues		Strong states' issues (Dominant factor loading)		Weak states' issues Non-dominant factor loading	
	(1)	(2)	(3)	(4)	(5)	(6)
Second period	3.03	3.25	2.67	2.96	6.18***	5.44***
	(3.29)	(3.27)	(3.49)	(3.57)	(2.07)	(1.99)
Constant	80.3***	83.3***	89.7***	93.1***	63.8***	65.5***
	(7.23)	(7.90)	(10.5)	(11.3)	(7.92)	(7.45)
Random effects:						
Issue salience	0.55**	0.59*	0.00	0.00	0.87**	0.92**
	(0.16)	(0.16)	(0.001)	(0.001)	(0.17)	(0.15)
Issue intercept	11.2***	11.2***	12.1***	12.2***	9.20***	8.98***
	(2.31)	(2.33)	(3.59)	(3.58)	(2.68)	(2.69)
N	3087	3087	2051	2051	1036	1036
Clusters (Issues)	25	25	15	15	10	10
Log-likelihood	−13831.3	−13826.6	−9151.7	−9148.3	−4667.9	−4666.4

Notes: The first part of the table reports the coefficients from a random-intercept-and-slope linear model of the continuous bargaining success measure (robust standard errors are in parentheses). The second part of the table refers to the random effects parameters and reports the standard deviation component estimates and errors for the level-2 covariates (issue intercepts and issue salience). The likelihood ratio test statistic for the null hypothesis that there is no cross-issue variation in bargaining success is rejected across all models. * $p < .1$, ** $p < .05$, *** $p < .01$.

find that salience is an even stronger predictor of success over these issues compared to Model 1. Importantly, however, I fail to detect a statistically significant effect of the interaction with climate risk. While the interaction in Model 4 has a similar coefficient estimate as Model 2, the confidence interval is larger and makes the prediction less reliable. So, according to this model, climate vulnerability fails to have a relevant effect on success over topics naturally and historically most applicable to strong states.

By contrast, Models 5 and 6 report the results for the subset of issues that lay outside the dominant latent dimensions of collective preferences, that is, the issues one could consider associated to weak states. The findings are notably different compared to Models 3–4. I find that salience in itself has little power in predicting success on weak states' issues, suggesting a more ambiguous effect of salience on the more dispersed topics on the UNFCCC agenda. However, the interaction between salience and vulnerability in Model 6 is positive and statistically significant. So, given a certain level of salience for the issues under consideration, objective vulnerability seems to yield success to the most committed countries – hence, weak countries at the climate negotiations. As delineated in the theory, the findings suggest that vulnerability provides volumes to the claims of actors caring for issues outside the core agenda of strong, industrialized countries.

The results from the interactions in Model 4 and 6 are further illustrated by the plots in Figure 4.3. The figure shows that – despite the relatively small point estimate effect – the implications of the interactions are not trivial. With regards to weak states' issues, countries that move from low risk to high risk on the climate vulnerability scale could spend only 20 percent (or more) of their National Communications on a topic to eventually see a relatively preferable international agreement on said topic. Substantively, the results remain unaltered if I measure success in a binary way or if I drop the potentially more endogenous covariates. The findings are also robust if I control for democracy and government ideology or if I use the alternate measure of vulnerability discussed earlier (see Appendix). In sum, the aggregate results provide support for the theory that weak states elicit power to settle international agreement not only from their intrinsic perseverance (salience) but also from larger claims linked to their objective, physical vulnerability to climate change.

4.2.2 Issue-by-Issue Analysis of Bargaining Outcomes

The set of analyses presented thus far offers some proof that conventionally powerless countries reach meaningful levels of success at international climate negotiations when their international vulnerability and domestic salience

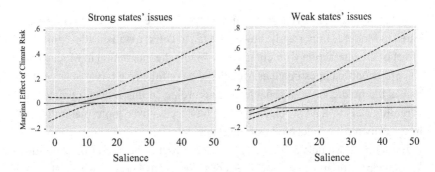

Figure 4.3 The conditional effect of climate risk on bargaining success

Notes: The figures show the interaction plots of salience moderating the effect of climate risk on bargaining success. The estimates correspond to the results of the interaction models in Table 4.1.

overlap. However, the statistical evidence is aggregated across issues, roughly divided across "strong states" and "weak states" issues. Here I present results that seek to provide a more fine-grained, issue-by-issue corroboration of my theory.

Leveraging the spatial structure of my data, I here propose a so-called Nash Bargaining Solution (NBS) analysis. This approach is based on Nash's game-theoretic framework of cooperation, and is regularly employed to study international cooperation outcomes based on spatial data.[25] In its essence, an NBS analysis involves reducing information about multiple parties (i.e., the UNFCCC countries' positions) into one single "solution." Empirically, the solution can be calculated following basic spatial assumptions. The negotiations' set of possible agreements is defined as a continuous vector where movement from the status quo implies an improvement toward more cooperation. The further away a bargaining outcome (O_j) is from each country's ideal point (x_{ij}), the larger a country's bargaining loss. Mathematically, the NBS equation is the maximization of the distance between countries' ideal point of cooperation to the actual collective bargaining outcome, minus the distance between the status quo (d_j) and the ideal position. Equation 4.2 reports this equation in Euclidean nomination.

$$NBS_j = \max_{O \in \Theta} \prod_{i=1}^{n} \left(-\sqrt{(O_j - x_{ij})^2} + \sqrt{(d_j - x_{ij})^2} \right) \qquad (4.2)$$

---

[25] Notable international relations works that make use of some form of NBS include Mansfield et al., 2000 and Thomson et al., 2006.

Importantly, the NBS can be altered. For example, one can add parameters (e.g., discount factors) to the basic equation. Consequently, differently computed NBS point estimates can be directly compared and easily adjudicated based on the weight of their different parameters. This is precisely what I do in this section, for the NBS calculated for each single UNFCCC issue. Specifically, I compare two types of NBS models: one that integrates only the weight of countries' issue salience, and one that also integrates the level of vulnerability (CRI) of each country. Following my theory, I expect the latter NBS calculations to be more accurate (less error-driven) for the issues associated to more vulnerable countries. Thus, following this reasoning, the CRI-weighted NBS should be more accurate at predicting the real UNFCCC outcomes on the issues evaluated earlier in this Element, where weak countries are assumed to have more morally compelling preferences in the eyes of domestic strong states audiences.

Estimation-wise, the first baseline NBS model is one with the integration of a salience factor. Specifically, I weigh individual preferences by *salience*, and then multiply the product to the maximand of the NBS. Equation 4.3 represents this NBS model with all the described parameters, which for my purposes are all standardized on a scale between 0 and 1.

$$NBS_j = \max_{O \in \Theta} \prod_{i=1}^{n} salience_{ij} * \left(-\sqrt{(O_j - x_{ij})^2} + \sqrt{(d_{ij} - x_{ij})^2} \right) \qquad (4.3)$$

I compare this to an asymmetric NBS calculated where the salience-discounted preferences are weighted by my indicator of vulnerability. Practically, just like the applied literature does to estimate the weight of other sources of international influence (Thomson & Stockman, 2006; Schneider et al., 2010), the vulnerability measure is introduced in the NBS objective function as an exponent. I assume a proportional relationship between countries' ideal positions, x_i, and their *vulnerability*$_i$, according to which a constant change in the weighted difference between the disagreement point and the observed outcome reflects the same proportional change in the NBS prediction. The collective maximization problem then corresponds to the equation:

$$NBS_j = \max_{O \in \Theta} \prod_{i=1}^{n} \left(salience_{ij} * \left(-\sqrt{(O_j - x_{ij})^2} + \sqrt{(d_j - x_{ij})^2} \right) \right)^{vulnerability_i}$$

$$(4.4)$$

I perform the calculations for all issues coded in my dataset minus the binary issues, because in yes–no decisions the assumption that all parties can settle on efficient cooperation cannot hold and the NBS inevitably halts on the status quo. So, in total, I calculate 38 outcomes for the baseline model (Equation 4.3) and the vulnerability model (equation 4.4).[26] The most informative metric of the relative performance of the NBS models is the absolute difference of the true outcome from the estimated outcome, that is, the models' issue-specific "absolute error."[27] The smaller the absolute error, the larger the accuracy of the model. Consequently, evaluating my hypothesis implies comparing the absolute errors of the predictions of the symmetric and asymmetric equations and determining to what extent they differ. In order to include uncertainty in the outcome predictions, which could be due, for example, to measurement problems, I simulate the standard deviation of each NBS point estimate. For my theory to be accurate, the asymmetric NBS model should perform better at predicting the issues discussed in Figure 4.1, in that for those issues the errors should be statistically smaller and closer to zero than the errors of the baseline model.

Figure 4.4 reports the main results. In the illustration, the absolute error estimates for the issues loading on the most dominant dimensions of the negotiations are on the left of the dotted vertical line. By contrast, the issues loading on the non-dominant factors, that is, the issues presumably more tilted toward weak states, are on the right of the vertical line. The grey squares represent the error estimates of the baseline model vis-à-vis the true observed outcome. The red crosses represent the error estimates of the model geared to test the relevance of vulnerability. I find that the baseline, salience-only NBS predicts well the international agreements on the more mitigation-related issues. For example, this model is better at predicting outcomes such as the decisions over the criteria of *CDM engagement* and on whether the UNFCCC should have *binding commitments*, in other words, issues that regard developed Annex I countries more closely.

Equally importantly for my theory, I find that the vulnerability-weighted model systematically outperforms the baseline on a number of topics that largely correspond to less mitigation-oriented issues. Specifically, the NBS that integrates the climate risk measure more accurately estimates 9 out of 13 non-mitigation oriented issues, including the decisions on *land use and forestry* (i.e., issues related to land use and forestry) and terms of accreditation of offset projects. This model also fares better than the baseline NBS model in predicting the cooperation achieved with respect to *nuclear energy*. The estimates are less sparse for the second period, mainly due to the strong effect that the status quo

---

[26] This makes my test more conservative, given that several yes–no issues in my dataset refer to altering normative language in the Convention, such as modifying the principle of supplementarity or moving away from the historical but differentiated responsibility principle. These issues largely resolved on the position of developing countries.

[27] The actual predicted outcomes are reported in the Appendix.

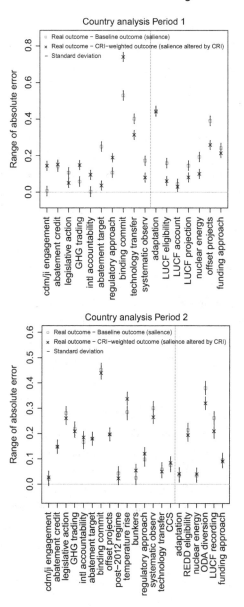

Figure 4.4 Issue-by-issue analysis of bargaining outcome estimations

Notes: The plots report the absolute errors of the estimations of bargaining outcomes via two country-level NBS models – the salience-based model (squares) and the asymmetric model where positions and salience are weighted by the Climate Risk Index (crosses). The black lines around the error estimates report the two standard deviations from each estimated issue-specific outcome. The vertical dotted line separates the issues loaded on the principal component dimension (see Figure 4.1) and those that are not.

had around the Copenhagen negotiations. However, even in Period 2 the CRI model outperforms the salience-only model in predicting the true outcome of the *ODA eligibility* of climate projects and other Land Use Change and Forestry (LUCF) issues (see right panel of the figure). Interestingly, vulnerability does not seem to improve the prediction of the collective outcome on the issue of adaptation funding.

Are these results in line with the moral legitimacy argument envisioned in my theory? A qualitative inspection of country-specific positions seems to suggest so. For example, developing countries have often raised the terms of use of nuclear energy when discussing "capacity to abate." Along these lines, in 2004 the Maldives government, supported by a number of Sub-Saharan countries, suggested a "wish to appl[y] concepts of preventive environmental management" because it was concerned with the use of "unsafe energy" (NC2, l. 2923). Most developed countries did not back up internationally standardized measures on how and whether to include nuclear power in their energy mix in view of emissions abatement. However, some of them (e.g., Canada) eventually adapted to their request of more standardization of how much nuclear power would be expected in the future, for domestic publics and NGOs started putting pressure on their responsibility on the issue, for example, of nuclear security and waste (Hultman, 2011). So, in line with my theory, the influence of small states on this issue was at least in part due to lobbying and framing efforts by domestic groups in strong states.[28]

While this set of results show additional support to the hypothesis of weak states' power at climate negotiations, it is possible that these predictions are a function of data features and measurement errors. For example, some scholars suggest that asymmetric NBS models may underperform when actors' preferences range between many proposals (Bueno De Mesquita, 2011). But even if this was the case because, for example, these models are more prone to so-called "corner" solutions, the vulnerability NBS model would still be useful at predicting more extreme negotiation cases, which presumably is the type of bargaining when the salience of small, vulnerable countries is most at stake.

It is worth noting that the NBS results are overall similar if I use the other, vulnerability-like measure to weigh the bargaining parameters of the asymmetric model. Specifically, I find that the absolute errors of the ODA-weighted model fares better than the baseline model on 9 out of the 12 issues identified as "weak states-relevant." For example, the ODA model generates smaller

---

[28] See also *Daedalus*, 2009. *Nuclear energy in developing countries.* www.amacad.org/publication/nuclear-energy-developing-countries. Last accessed on May 19, 2020.

errors for most LUCF issues, which heavily rely on the preferences of developing countries. This is in line with other analyses that suggest that high ODA receiving countries decide when and how to provide natural carbon sinks *if* – following the principle of fairness – they are given the opportunity to satisfy their basic development needs (Favero & De Cian, 2010).

Additionally, some of the main results are qualitatively similar if the analyses are run at the *coalition* instead of national levels. Group alliances do matter a great deal in international organizations, and states often align with the position of their coalition (Johnson & Urpelainen, 2012). In the case of the UNFCCC, several studies mention the influence of coalitions and coalition-building as a way to increase power (Chasek, 2005; Betzold, 2010), although it is also noted that coalitions have fragmented across time, potentially losing effectiveness in recent years (Ourbak & Magnan, 2018). For my purposes, using the distribution of positions at the coalition level may provide more variance across the NBS predictions. Furthermore, exploring the results at the coalition level may be useful to know if the interaction of vulnerability and salience holds also at this degree of aggregation.

To check the sensitivity of my main results to coalition preferences, I combine the data at the level of UNFCCC Party Groupings, which include the Umbrella Group, the Environmental Integrity Group, the EU, and the Group of 77 (G77).[29] The results compare the baseline outcome predictions with the estimates from the EPI-based model (see Appendix for the models). Once again, the asymmetric model predicts with meaningful accuracy the decisions made on issues that evoke concerns with fairness, such as the negotiations related to *LUCF* and *emission abatement targets*. The issue of multilateral funding (*funding approach*) is also well predicted by the vulnerability NBS with a relatively small error, indicating that the G77 may have determined the agreement on this issue, at least in later negotiation years. Overall, these additional findings provide further evidence that developing countries have a substantial influence over what would seem to be the issues they "own" at the UNFCCC.[30]

---

[29] I do not refine the G77 analysis into the sub-groups that make up the G77 such as the AOSIS and the LDC group due to limited National Communications on that front.

[30] The average errors of the asymmetric model improve for the second period, perhaps to indicate that in the 2008–2011 years coalitions better represented interests at the UNFCCC. At the same time and more generally, the evidence indicates that my argument holds for both aggregated and more fine-grained (nation-level) analyses, and that the results are not sensitive to the fact that some countries in coalitions such as the AOSIS have deviated from their group positions (Ourbak & Magnan, 2018).

4.3 Mechanisms: The Catalysts of Weak States' Political Leverage in Strong Countries

The results in the previous section have two implications for the influence of weak states at international climate meetings. First, the findings indicate that less powerful states' sole efforts to push their favorite agreement at climate negotiations is hardly a winning strategy. Alone, concern for an issue is not sufficient for weak states to attain bargaining outcomes, while it may serve the utility of more powerful, developed nations. At the same time, the results indicate that the domestic urgency that weak states attach to UNFCCC issues is conducive to bargaining success if they are objectively vulnerable to climate change. As I have argued, the risk of being a victim of the effects of climate change seems to constitute an important condition for international powers to take these states' preferences seriously. Hence, these findings are in line with the conjecture that the domestic politics of strong states and, in particular, internal debates about vulnerability and their implications for leadership play a crucial role to legitimize the positions of weak states at the UNFCCC.

In this section I attempt to dive more into the mechanisms envisioned by the theory, to provide further evidence for the sources of moral legitimacy of weak states' issues in strong states besides the aforementioned anecdotes. I concentrate specifically on two domestic sources that the literature unambiguously considers relevant to influence leadership (Risse et al., 1999; Simmons, 2009) and to frame foreign affairs priorities in developed countries (Weeks, 2008; Prakash & Gugerty, 2010). I focus first on the lobbying action of NGOs at international negotiations and its framing effects. I then delineate the connection between climate vulnerability, global justice, and concern with climate action in *public opinion*, using the United Kingdom as the primary example.

4.3.1 Framing (and Shaming) by Non-governmental Organizations at the UNFCCC

The international relations scholarship has documented the massive growth in subnational actors, and in particular private and public NGOs, involved in environmental politics over the last two decades (Bulkeley et al., 2014). It is reported that these groups have undertaken a variety of governance functions, in part also to put in track the debate at the international negotiations (Hoffmann, 2011). In particular, it is argued that these actors have been influential at exchanging information with the public and framing concerns otherwise marginal to the core negotiation set (Andonova et al., 2009). In line with the argument delineated in this Element, the NGOs based in developed countries have had a critical focus on issues of vulnerability in developing countries in recent years (Allan & Hadden, 2017).

To interrogate this conjecture, I explore the content of submissions of a selection of NGOs nominally based in rich countries and active at the UNFCCC annual meetings. Specifically, I investigate the topics in the speeches that these NGOs officially presented at the international climate meetings made between 2008 and 2011. I limit the analysis to these years because "observer (NGO) participation" at the Conference of the Parties was only allowed starting in 2007, and also because these years roughly correspond to those analyzed earlier in this Element.[31]

The NGO submissions to the UNFCCC come with some limitations. The submitting observers need to apply in order to register their participation at the annual meetings, and the Executive Secretary has the discretion to admit participants following the successful completion of the admission process. This implies that the selected observers are not representative of the universe of NGOs involved in the UNFCCC process. However, this works in my favor for the purposes of this analysis, for most of the submissions (>85 percent) are from organizations headquartered in OECD countries, that is, the countries in which I expect the moral account of vulnerable countries' issues to resonate the most. In total, I collected fifty-one statements from forty-seven NGOs (only four presented more than one statement in the four observed years). The statements are not standardized but are relatively short (average length: 1,750 words circa). This means that each document can only be focused on a handful of topics, and more generally concentrated on one or two maximum. If NGOs at the UNFCCC indeed constitute a framing channel that puts the issues of the most vulnerable countries in the face of the most developed countries, then a significant portion of these texts should be dedicated to these issues.

To identify the topics in the NGO submissions, I employ a topic model that assumes that each document consists of a mixture of topics, and that each topic is a mixture of words. After basic pre-processing, I establish that a conscript of topics captures the major themes of the NGOs. To maximize interpretability, I settle on four topics. I then calculate the model following a classic Latent Dirichlet Allocation (LDA) specification (Blei et al., 2003). For my purposes, I first describe the distribution of the topics identified across all texts. I then zoom in on the topics of a selection of the most influential participating NGOs.

---

[31] For an analysis of NGO discourse during the Paris Agreement negotiations, see Allan & Hadden (2017).

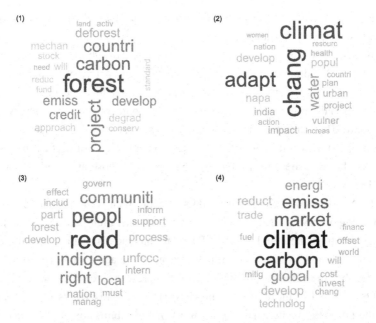

Words in "Forest Emissions & Carbon Projects" topic (upper left), "Adaptation" topic (upper right)
"REDD & Communities" topic (lower left), and "Market" topic (lower right)

Figure 4.5 Wordclouds of most probable words in each of four estimated NGO topics

Notes: This plot visualizes the twenty most probable words in each of the four topics estimated for the environmental non-governmental organization (ENGO) statements submitted to the UNFCCC between 2008 and 2011.

Figure 4.5 shows the word clouds capturing the 10 most probable words of each inferred topic, where larger and smaller fonts represent a higher and lower frequency, respectively.[32] The first topic rotates around the words *forest*, *credit*, and *project*; these terms hint to (de)forestation, carbon sinks, and abatement credits projects, all of which are hosted in developing countries. The second topic focuses on *adaptation*, *water*, as well as *vulnerability*, and seems to capture issues of adaptation impact and other tangential climate action related to vulnerable countries. The third topic is more tilted to issues of *community* and *indigenous* people; again, these seem to be especially relevant to the less resilient countries of the world. Only the fourth topic concentrates on issues that appear more salient to mitigation in rich industrialized countries, that is, *emission markets* and *technology development*. Altogether, this plot indicates that

---

[32] The most probable terms from each of the topic are identified by sorting the term-topic-probability vector in decreasing order.

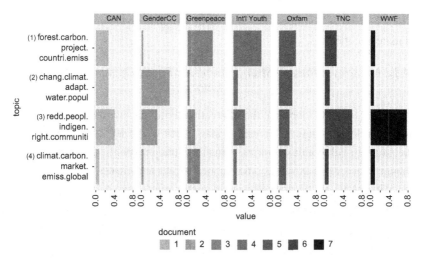

Figure 4.6 Topic proportions for most representative ENGOs at the UNFCCC

Notes: This figure visualizes the topic distributions within the documents of a selected number of ENGOs based on the four-topic model estimation.

NGOs discussing at the UNFCCC are heavily focused on issues very salient to developing, vulnerable countries. This suggests that NGOs at the UNFCCC are significantly committed to magnify the concerns of weak countries and keep world leaders accountable for action (or inaction) over them. Evidence from the framing effect of NGOs at more recent conferences suggests a similar pattern, with significant concentration on issues of loss and damage (Vanhala & Hestbaek, 2016).

To provide further evidence, Figure 4.6 shows the histograms of the topic proportion calculated for the seven most influential NGOs (inferred by number of members as of 2011), which include the Climate Action Network (CAN), the International Youth Climate Movement (IYCM) and the World Wildlife Fund (WWF). All parameters for this subgroup analysis are set to fit the data and provide the highest overall probability of the model. Accordingly, all seven NGOs cover at least a small percentage of each of the four identified topic. However, the topics that dominate the vast majority of these documents are the ones attached to issues of weak countries (Topic 1–3). In fact, only for Greenpeace the topic of carbon emissions is significantly prominent. This is again suggestive of the pressure that NGOs put on governments at the UNFCCC, and specifically their home executives on which they have more direct lobbying power. Coupled with evidence that governments do pay attention to these actors, this information sheds light on one meaningful mechanism through which vulnerable countries have consistently elicited power at the international climate negotiations.

4.3.2 Mass Awareness in Strong Countries: Public Opinion in the United Kingdom

In parallel to NGO lobbying, the international politics literature indicates that another relevant source of pressure that forces world leaders to concede to the issues of vulnerable countries stems from national public opinion. Climate change exacerbates existing domestic inequalities and creates new dimensions for political debate. Historically, developing nations have carried the brunt of climate change impacts (Ciplet et al., 2015). However, in recent years developed countries have increasingly started feeling the consequences more closely, too (Bechtel & Hainmueller, 2011; Obradovich et al., 2018). These experiences, one may argue, have deeply affected how the public relates to climate change-induced events, and what connections people in rich countries make between climate change impacts, the international claims of weak countries, and the distribution of global power overall.

While the literature still debates the political relevance of experiencing climate disasters (Egan & Mullin, 2012; Bergquist & Warshaw, 2019), it seems at least plausible that people in the developed world, who experience natural disasters may be more likely to connect their experience to the conditions of people in poorer, more vulnerable states (Konisky et al., 2016). This shared experience could concomitantly cause a preference for more fair configurations of global wealth redistribution, just like distributive justice emerges in related to affectedness and need-based conceptions of fairness (Gasper & Reeves, 2011; Bechtel et al., 2014). If this connection were to be true, then the hypothesis that developed countries concede power to more vulnerable ones following domestic political pressure would have even more validity, because the participation in the "sufferance" of climate vulnerability could give momentum to feelings about global fairness and redistribution, and these could strengthen even further beliefs about vulnerable countries' legitimate requests.

To get at this mechanism, I focus on publicly available opinion data from the United Kingdom (UK). I choose the United Kingdom because it is a developed country with important stakes in global environmental politics. Its public debate over climate change also has fewer caveats compared to other countries. For example, differently from the United States, UK climate politics is less entrenched in bipartisanship and media trust in climate science. Additionally, in the winter of 2013–2014 the United Kingdom saw a series of severe storms that led to a major emergency response and extensive media exposure. These winter floods offer an opportunity to examine how the UK public engaged with broad questions around climate politics after these events.

Exploiting this opportunity, Demski et al. (2017) fielded a survey to individuals personally affected by flooding (200 interviews for 5 flood affected areas, so N = 1,000) and, in parallel, a nationally representative sample (N= 1,000). The questionnaire included a number of standard survey items, as well as more targeted political questions. My assumption is that individuals mostly affected by flooding would make the strongest connection between the status of climate vulnerable populations and more general issues of global justice and redistribution. Consequently, I expect these communities – which, arguably, take a lot of political space in the outset of a domestic climate crisis like a flood – to make a strong connection between climate vulnerability in weak countries (i.e., developing countries) and global justice.

I test this conjecture with the data at hand. For my dependent variable I operationalize the question *"How serious a threat, if at all, is climate change to people in developing countries?"*. This is scaled on five values from "Not Very Serious" to "Extremely Serious", although the results do not change if the variable is coded as 1 if the respondents answered "Extremely Serious" or "Serious," and 0 otherwise. I correlate the outcome to the response to the question *"To what extent do you agree or disagree with the statement; the world would be a better place if its wealth were divided equally among nations?"*. Here the variable takes the value of 1 if the respondents answered "Strongly Agree" or "Tend to Agree," and 0 otherwise. The analyses are based on a linear model with robust standard errors. I control for gender, age, education, as well as a binary measure of political ideology based on respondents' favored party at the time of the survey. The ideology measure causes a significant drop in observations, however the results are robust – and in fact statistically stronger – if I exclude this covariate from the analysis (see Appendix). Furthermore, the results are not sensitive to weight adjustments.

I present the results in two fashions: first, I show the correlation between the responses to the two questions by sample; then, I show the interaction effect between the flooded sample and opinion about global justice. Table 4.2 shows three models: one for the aggregate sample, one for the UK national sample (the benchmark), and one for the highly salient flooded areas sample. According to Model 1, British respondents who are most sensitive to global justice also tend to believe that climate change is a serious threat to people in developing countries. However, this correlation is not statistically driven by the UK average respondent, as shown by the lack of statistical significance

Table 4.2 Vulnerability, equality and global climate concerns: a UK analysis

	Y: "Climate change is a serious threat to people in developing countries"		
	All respondents	UK national sample	UK flooded areas sample
	(1)	(2)	(3)
"The world would be better if wealth	0.108***	0.066	0.115***
was divided equally among nations"	(0.026)	(0.040)	(0.038)
Female	0.067	−0.018	0.034
	(0.060)	(0.092)	(0.100)
Age: 18 to 24	0.230	−0.386	0.496
	(0.343)	(0.479)	(0.366)
Age: 25 to 34	0.219	−0.370	0.451
	(0.345)	(0.487)	(0.365)
Age: 35 to 44	0.467	−0.476	0.930***
	(0.339)	(0.478)	(0.358)
Age: 45 to 54	0.329	−0.401	0.788**
	(0.338)	(0.481)	(0.351)
Age: 55 to 64	0.549	−0.144	0.991***
	(0.338)	(0.481)	(0.353)
Age: 65 to 74	0.470	−0.312	0.711**
	(0.339)	(0.490)	(0.356)
Age: 75 to 80	0.334	−0.190	0.669*
	(0.357)	(0.508)	(0.391)
Age: above 80	0.413	−0.401	0.654*
	(0.349)	(0.505)	(0.383)
Education: GCSE	0.313***	0.273	0.222
	(0.117)	(0.174)	(0.172)
Education: Vocational	0.317**	0.040	0.294
	(0.141)	(0.199)	(0.209)
Education: A-level	0.220*	0.135	0.268
	(0.117)	(0.169)	(0.170)
Education: Bachelors	0.409***	0.141	0.560***
	(0.110)	(0.168)	(0.157)

Education:	0.579***	0.514***	0.514***
MA-Bachelors	(0.120)	(0.185)	(0.164)
Education: Still	0.635***	0.306*	0.000
studying (university)	(0.156)	(0.173)	(0.000)
Education: Other	0.329**	−0.176	0.581***
qualification	(0.140)	(0.209)	(0.203)
Ideology: Left	0.269***	0.204**	0.248**
	(0.063)	(0.101)	(0.099)
Constant	−0.317	2.469**	−0.338
	(0.794)	(1.191)	(1.025)
Observations	1,027	515	512
R-squared	0.093	0.064	0.139

Notes: The table reports the coefficients from a linear model of the "Climate Threat" survey item that includes a dummy variable of political ideology (robust standard errors in parentheses). The reference categories are *Age: 16 to 18*, *Education: Primary Education only*, and *Ideology: Right*. The third column refers to the oversampled of residents in Dawlish, Hull, West London (Windsor-Sunbury), Tewksbury and Gloucester, and Aberystwyth (Ceredigion). Weights are included in the analysis. * $p < .1$, ** $p < .05$, *** $p < .01$.

in Model 2. Rather, the strong connection between global fairness and concern with climate vulnerability abroad is driven by people who experienced climate risks via flooding, as indicated by Model 3. The interaction effect reported in Table 4.3 corroborates this result: Here I find that, conditional on respondents having some sensitivity to the global justice issue, being flooded magnifies public concern about the impact of climate change in weak countries abroad. In other words, communities politicized over climate change have strong opinions in favor of international redistribution that also encompasses protection of vulnerable countries. This is in line with my argument that domestic salience and vulnerability at home can be plausibly connected to why salience and vulnerability of weak countries predict their success at the UNFCCC.

This public opinion evidence also falls in line with other research that finds that people explicitly want their government's leaders to provide more international compensation in the aftermath of natural disasters, especially if they are sensitive to fairness norms of distributive justice (Bechtel & Mannino, 2019). All in all, the evidence illustrates that important fractions embedded in the civil society of developed states can magnify the legitimacy of issues

Table 4.3 Vulnerability, equality, and global climate concerns: interaction model

	Y: "Climate change is a serious threat to people in developing countries"
"The world would be better if wealth was divided equally among nations"	0.024 (0.018)
UK flooded area	−0.176** (0.088)
"The world would be better if wealth was divided equally among nations" × UK flooded area	0.040* (0.023)
Sex	✓
Age	✓
Education	✓
Ideology	✓
Constant	0.157 (0.162)
Observations	1,027
R-squared	0.065

Notes: The table reports the coefficients from a linear model of the "Climate Threat" survey item (robust standard errors in parentheses). * $p < .1$, ** $p < .05$, *** $p < .01$.

of vulnerable countries, thereby providing them with more moral power at international climate negotiations.

5 Conclusion

5.1 Power at International Climate Negotiations: A Summary

Refraining climate change is an important question increasingly engrossing leaders around the globe. However, the worldwide costs of accelerating decarbonization are highly imbalanced. "Strong" developed countries are historically responsible for accumulation of global greenhouse gases. Vice versa, the most dramatic climate change-induced events are experienced by the highly "weak," vulnerable countries. According to a realist view, these disparities would suggest that strong countries possess the resources to solve the problem, and are thus in charge of deciding the shape and pace of global climate policies. By contrast, weak countries are left at the sideline of climate negotiations, incapable of shifting the discourse, or credibly act against the will of the strong.

Yet, the past two decades of UNFCCC negotiations point to the bargaining success of minor states, from benchmarking numbers for adaptation funds to setting terms on some carbon credit programs. While these victories have implied no significant reduction of climate change, they have had relevant political repercussions. At the outset of a number of UN climate negotiations, several Global South nations have made the international news as champions of the negotiation process. Their leaders have equally earned domestic gains from this international clout. These anecdotes beg the question: what determines the soft but consistent power of minor states at international climate negotiations?

The most common argument put forward to explain these examples of negotiation success is built around the domestic actors within weak states. Accordingly, these are able to mobilize around the existential issue of climate change to the point of coordinating salience and trumping stronger countries' interests. However, this argument is increasingly challenged by the fact that on several issues strong states seem to simply concede power without weak states requiring too much coordination. The argument also implies a large effort of domestic preference mobilization in weak states that lacks empirical evidence.

In this Element I put forward an alternate argument, which seeks to combine both the earlier realist take and the domestic politics view of power balance at international climate negotiations. On the one hand, I maintain that strong states hold the agenda-setting power at international climate conferences, and control the issues that are most naturally relevant to their economies. On the other hand, I contend that weak states assert power on certain UNFCCC issues as a combination of their domestic salience over them *and* the moral authority elicited by their objective climate vulnerability. My argument underlines the role that discourse and framing of vulnerability has within *strong states* and their implications on strong countries' leadership. My theory suggests that, on issues naturally catered to the conditions of weak countries, the higher the level of climate vulnerability experienced by given countries, the more strong countries' leaders are domestically pressured to provide to their requests. Hence, in those circumstances the weak states' positions would determine the ultimate negotiation outcome over those issues.

In support of the theory, I supplied evidence obtained using several data and various methodological approaches. I first tested the macro implications of the theory on an original dataset I collected for national preference and salience over a large number of issues discussed at the UNFCCC negotiations between 2001 and 2011. I analyze the data both in their aggregate and issue-by-issue, to both quantitatively and qualitative evaluate on which issues the combination of objective vulnerability and issue salience play in the favor of weak states' bargaining power. The findings are largely in favor of my argument that salience per se is not enough at predicting influence of marginal nation states at climate negotiations. Rather, salience combined with objective measures of climate vulnerability provides more precise and significant predictions of weak states' influence at the global climate negotiations.

I additionally explored the underlying logic that actors within strong states facilitate weak states' power via framing their requests around their legitimate concerns of vulnerability and climate risk. In particular, I showed how NGOs participating at the UNFCCC and public opinion in some influential global powers actively connect the climate policy issues of the developing world with concerns of climate change vulnerability. This evidence indicates how these forces are in support of magnifying foreign countries' issues in name of international redistribution and world fairness. While these results on their own cannot yield irrefutable proof of the theory's claims, they provide some new insights in line with the logic that strong states' domestic politics are critical determinants of the role weak states take at international climate negotiations.

5.2 Contributions to Climate Politics Research and Implications for International Relations

The framework presented in this Element adds to the knowledge of different realms of international politics research. First, the theory asserts the crucial role of domestic politics (and actors) in pivoting transnational conversations about climate policy, which the environmental political science literature has only recently started exploring. My argument provides a new angle on how national leaders in strong countries can be forced to pledge action on the diffused area of climate policy when they would otherwise not seem to be directly interested. Additionally, the study defends the importance of investigating the interlinkage between climate concerns and other issues related to international redistribution and global justice. By bringing in the intuition of moral legitimacy of climate-vulnerable places, the study seeks to contribute to the growing scholarship that focuses on the political effects of perception and exposure to climate risks.

The research also sheds light on other persistent puzzles in international relations. The theory facilitates an understanding of when the dominant states in an international organization force their preferences on others and when, alternately, they decide to *refrain* from investing in coercive diplomacy. As argued in this Element, this is more likely when they are aware of lacking moral authority and sense the possibility of political backlash at home. Along these lines, while scholars have examined the conditions that lead states to increase diplomatic efforts dictated by domestic salience on international issues, they have paid less attention to the conditions that make domestic salience more legitimate – be this objective climate change risk or other types of vulnerability.

Finally, this research speaks to the role of international institutions in the global system. Although some scholars assume that these bodies of international order are mostly shaped by strong countries, few still appreciate the implications these may have on locking strong states in certain types of commitments or potentially exposing them to naming and shaming at home. The findings hence inform debates over leadership in international relations and the design of international institutions, suggesting some of the motivations that some strong states have to maintain international negotiations at a certain form and pace. On the one hand, this study indicates the impossibility of truly challenging the historical power of strong states and their ever still crucial role in international politics. On the other hand, I showed evidence for why the historical "outsides" of international regimes can capitalize on dynamics within the global powers to obtain political victories, and how they can shape in their favor at least part of the global agenda on issues they have credible stakes on.

References

Abbott, Kenneth W. & Snidal, Duncan. 1998. Why States Act through Formal International Organizations. *The Journal of Conflict Resolution*, **42**(1), 3–32.

Abbott, Kenneth W. & Snidal, Duncan. 2000. Hard and Soft Law in International Governance. *International Organization*, **54**(3), 421–456.

Adger, W. N. 2001. Scales of Governance and Environmental Justice for Adaptation and Mitigation of Climate Change. *Journal of International development*, **13**, 921–931.

Ahmed, S. A., Diffenbaugh, N. S., & Hertel, T. 2009. Climate Volatility Deepens Poverty Vulnerability in Developing Countries. *Environmental Research Letters*, **4**:1–8.

Allan, Jen Iris & Hadden, Jennifer. 2017. Exploring the Framing Power of NGOs in Global Climate Politics. *Environmental Politics*, **26**(4), 600–620.

Andonova, Liliana B., Betsill, Michele M., & Bulkeley, Harriet. 2009. Transnational Climate Governance. *Global Environmental Politics*, **9**(2), 52–73.

Andresen, S. & Agrawala, S. 2002. Leaders, Pushers and Laggards in the Making of the Climate Regime. *Global Environmental Change*, **12**, 41–51.

Arregui, J. & Thomson, R. 2009. States' Bargaining Success in the European Union. *Journal of European Public Policy*, **16**(5), 655–676.

Ashe, J., Lierop, R. V., and Cherian, A. 1999. The Role of the Alliance of Small Island States (AOSIS) in the Negotiation of the United Nations Framework Convention on Climate Change (UNFCCC). *Natural Resource Forum*, **23**(3), 209–220.

Axelrod, R. 1997. *The Complexity of Cooperation: Agent-Based Models of Competition and Collaboration*. Princeton University Press.

Bailer, S. 2004. Bargaining Success in the European Union. *European Union Politics*, **5**(1), 99–123.

Bankoff, Greg, Frerks, Georg, & Hilhorst, Dorothea. 2013. *Mapping Vulnerability: Disasters, Development, and People*. Routledge.

Barrett, S. 2007. *Why Cooperate? The Incentive to Supply Global Public Goods*. Oxford University Press, USA.

Barrett, S. & Stavins, R. 2003. Increasing Participation and Compliance in International Climate Change Agreements. *International Environmental Agreements: Politics, Law and Economics*, **3**(4), 349–376.

Bauer, S. 2006. Does Bureaucracy Really Matter? The Authority of Intergovernmental Treaty Secretariats in Global Environmental Politics. *Global Environmental Politics*, **6**(1), 23–49.

Bayer, P. & Urpelainen, J. 2013. Funding Global Public Goods: The Dark Side of Multilateralism. *Review of Policy Research*, **30**(2), 160–189.

Bechtel, Michael M. & Hainmueller, Jens. 2011. How Lasting Is Voter Gratitude? An Analysis of the Short- and Long-Term Electoral Returns to Beneficial Policy. *American Journal of Political Science*, **55**(4), 851–867.

Bechtel, Michael M. & Mannino, Massimo. 2019. How Do Voters Judge Policy Responses to Natural Disasters? https://papers.ssrn.com/sol3/papers.cfm?abstract_id=2943046. Working Paper.

Bechtel, Michael M., Hainmueller, Jens, & Margalit, Yotam. 2014. Preferences for International Redistribution: The Divide over the Eurozone Bailouts. *American Journal of Political Science*, **58**(4), 835–856.

Bergquist, Parrish & Warshaw, Christopher. 2019. Does Global Warming Increase Public Concern about Climate Change? *The Journal of Politics*, **81**(2), 686–691.

Bernhagen, Patrick. 2008. Business and International Environmental Agreements: Business Influence over Participation and Compliance. *Global Environmental Politics*, **8**(1), 78–110.

Bernstein, S. & Hoffmann, M. 2018. The Politics of Decarbonization and the Catalytic Impact of Subnational Climate Experiments. *Policy Sciences*, **51**(2), 189–211.

Betsill, Michele & Corell, Elisabeth. 2008. *NGO Diplomacy: The Influence of Nongovernmental Organizations in International Environmental Negotiations*. Cambridge University Press.

Betzold, C. 2010. 'Borrowing' Power to Influence International Negotiations: AOSIS in the Climate Change Regime, 1990–1997. *Politics*, **20**(3), 131–148.

Betzold, C. & Weiler, F. 2017. Allocation of Aid for Adaptation to Climate Change: Do Vulnerable Countries Receive More Support? *International Environmental Agreements: Politics, Law and Economics*, **1**, 17–36.

Betzold, C. & Weiler, F. 2018. *Development Aid and Adaptation to Climate Change in Developing Countries*. Palgrave MacMillan.

Betzold, C., Castro, P., & Weiler, F. 2012. AOSIS in the UNFCCC Negotiations: From Unity to Fragmentation? *Climate Policy*, **12**(5), 519–613.

Binmore, K., Rubinstein, A., & Wolinsky, A. 1986. The Nash Bargaining Solution in Economic Modelling. *Rand Journal of Economics*, **17**(2), 176–188.

Bjoerkdahl, A. 2008. Norm Advocacy: A Small State Strategy to Influence the EU. *Journal of European Public Policy*, **15**(1), 135–154.

Blei, David M., Ng, Andrew Y., & Jordan, Michael I. 2003. Latent Dirichlet Allocation. *Journal of Machine Learning Research*, **3**, 993–1022.

Bodansky, D. 2010. The Copenhagen Climate Change Conference: A Post-mortem. *American Journal of International Law*, **104**(2), 230–240.

Bodansky, Daniel. 2012. The Durban Platform Negotiations: Goals and Options. Harvard Project on Climate Agreements Viewpoint. https://www.belfercenter.org/publication/durban-platform-negotiations-goals-and-options.

Boehringer, Christoph. 2014. Two Decades of European Climate Policy: A Critical Appraisal. *Review of Environmental Economics and Policy*, **8**(1), 1–17.

Boerzel, Tanja A. & Risse, Thomas. 2010. Governance without a State: Can it Work? *Regulation and Governance*, **4**(2), 113–134.

Böhmelt, Tobias. 2013. Civil Society Lobbying and Countries' Climate Change Policies: A Matching Approach. *Climate Policy*, **13**(6), 698–717.

Briguglio, L. 1995. Small Island Developing States and their Economic Vulnerabilities. *World Development*, **23**(9), 1615–1632.

Brown, Katrina & Corbera, Esteve. 2003. Exploring Equity and Sustainable Development in the New Carbon Economy. *Climate Policy*, **3**(1): S41–S56.

Buchanan, Allen & Keohane, Robert O. 2006. The Legitimacy of Global Governance Institutions. *Ethics & International Affairs*, **20**(4), 405–437.

Budge, Ian, Klingemann, H.-D., Volkens, A., Bara, J., & Tanenbaum, E. 2001. *Mapping Policy Preferences: Parties, Electors, and Governments, 1945-1998*. Oxford: Oxford University Press.

Bueno De Mesquita, B. 2011. A New Model for Predicting Policy Choices. *Conflict Management and Peace Science*, **28**(1), 65–87.

Bulkeley, Harriet, Andonova, L., Betsill, Michele M., et al. 2014. *Transnational Climate Change Governance*. Cambridge University Press.

Busby, J. W. 2010. *Moral Movements and Foreign Policy*. Cambridge: Cambridge University Press.

Busby, J. W. 2016. *Sustainable Security: Rethinking American National Security Strategy*. Oxford: Oxford University Press. Chap. "Climate Change and US National Security: Sustaining Security Admidst Unsustainability."

Carley, Sanya, Evans, Tom P., Graff, Michelle, & Konisky., David M. 2018. A Framework for Evaluating Geographic Disparities in Energy Transition Vulnerability. *Nature Energy*, **3**, 621–627.

Carnegie, Allison. 2014. States Held Hostage: Political Hold-Up Problems and the Effects of International Institutio. *American Political Science Review*, **108**(1), 54–70.

Chasek, P. S. 2005. Margins of Power: Coalition Building and Coalition Maintenance of the South Pacific Island States and the Alliance of Small Island

States. *Review of European Community and International Environmental Law*, **2**, 125–137.

Chasek, Pamela S. 2001. NGOs and State Capacity in International Environmental Negotiations: The Experience of the Earth Negotiations Bulletin. *Review of European Community and International Environmental Law*, **10**(2), 168–176.

Checkel, Jeffrey T. 1997. International Norms and Domestic Politics: Bridging the Rationalist – Constructivist Divide. *European Journal of International Relations*, **3**(4), 473–495.

Chong, Dennis & Druckman, James N. 2007. Framing Theory. *Annual Review of Political Science*, **10**, 103–126.

Ciplet, David, Roberts, J. Timmons, & Khan, Mizan R. 2015. *Power in a Warming World: The New Global Politics of Climate Change and the Remaking of Environmental Inequality*. MIT Press.

Dai, X. 2006. The Conditional Nature of Democratic Compliance. *Journal of Conflict Resolution*, **50**(5), 690–713.

Davis, Christina. 2009. Linkage Diplomacy: Economic and Security Bargaining in the Anglo-Japanese Alliance, 1902–23. *International Security*, **33**(3): 143–179.

de Agueda Corneloup, Ines, & Mol, Arthur P. J. 2014. Small Island Developing States and International Climate Change Negotiations: The Power of Moral "Leadership". *International Environmental Agreements*, **14**, 281–197.

Demski, C., Capstick, S., Pidgeon, N., Sposato, R. G., & Spence, A. 2017. Experience of Extreme Weather Affects Climate Change Mitigation and Adaptation Responses. *Climatic Change*, **140**, 149–164.

Depledge, J. 2008. Striving for No: Saudi Arabia in the Climate Change Regime. *Global Environmental Politics*, **8**(4), 9–35.

Dimitrov, R. 2010. Inside the UN Climate Change Negotiations: The Copenhagen Conference. *Review of Policy Research*, **27**(6), 759–821.

Dimitrov, Radoslav S. 2005. Hostage to Norms: States, Institutions and Global Forest Politics. *Global Environmental Politics*, **5**(4), 1–24.

Downs, George W. & Jones, M. A. 2002. Reputation, Compliance, and International Law. *Journal of Legal Studies*, **31**(Sq), S95–S114.

Drahos, P. 2003. When the Weak Bargain with the Strong: Negotiations in the World Trade Organization. *International Organization*, **8**(1), 79–109.

Dutschke, Michael & Michaelowa, Axel. 2006. Development Assistance and the CDM – How to Interpret "Financial Additionality". *Environment and Development Economics*, **11**(2), 235–246.

Easterly, William & Kraay, Aart. 2000. Small States, Small Problems? Income, Growth, and Volatility in Small States. *World Development*, **28**(11), 2013–2027.

Egan, P. J. & Mullin, M. 2012. Turning Personal Experience into Political Attitudes: The Effect of Local Weather on Americans' Perceptions about Global Warming. *The Journal of Politics*, **74**(3), 796–809.

Falkner, Robert, Stephan, Hannes, & Vogler, John. 2010. International Climate Policy after Copenhagen: Towards a "Building Blocks" Approach. *Global Policy*, **1**(3), 252–262.

Favero, Alice & De Cian, Enrica. 2010 (July). *Fairness, Credibility and Effectiveness in the Copenhagen Accord: An Economic Assessment*. Fondazione Eni Enrico Mattei Working Paper No. 21.2010.

Fearon, J. D. 1994. Domestic Political Audiences and the Escalation of International Disputes. *American Political Science Review*, **88**(3), 577–592.

Finnemore, Martha & Sikkink, Kathryn. 1998. International Norm Dynamics and Political Change. *International Organization*, **52**(4), 887–917.

Forsyth, Tim. 2007. Promoting the "Development Dividend" of Climate Technology Transfer: Can Cross-sector Partnerships Help? *World Development*, **35**(10), 1684–1698.

Franchino, F. 2000. Control of the Commission's Executive Functions: Uncertainty, Conflict and Decision Rules. *European Union Politics*, **1**(1), 59–88.

Fukuyama, Francis. 2004. *State-Building: Governance and World Order in the 21st Century*. Cornell University Press.

Garrett, G. 1992. International Cooperation and Institutional Choice: The European Community's Internal Market. *International Organization*, **46**(2), 533–560.

Gasper, John T. & Reeves, Andrew. 2011. Make It Rain? Retrospection and the Attentive Electorate in the Context of Natural Disasters. *American Journal of Political Science*, **55**(2).

Genovese, Federica. 2014. States' Interests and Bargaining Positions at the UN Climate Change Negotiations: Exploring a New Dataset. *Environmental Politics*, **23**(4), 610–631.

Genovese, Federica. 2019. Sectors, Pollution, and Trade: How Industrial Interests Shape Domestic Positions on Global Climate Agreements. *International Studies Quarterly*, **63**(4), 819–836.

Germanwatch. 2019. *Climate Risk Index*. Tech. rept. Germanwatch.

Grant, Ruth W. & Keohane, Robert O. 2005. Accountability and Abuses of Power in World Politics. *American Political Science Review*, **99**(1), 29–43.

Grasso, Marco. 2010. An Ethical Approach to Climate Adaptation Finance. *Global Environmental Change*, **20**(1), 74–81.

Greif, A., Milgrom, P., & Weingast, B. R. 1994. Coordination, Commitment, and Enforcement: The Case of the Merchant Guild. *The Journal of Political Economy*, **102**(4), 745.

Gupta, J. 2012. Negotiating Challenges and Climate Change. *Climate Policy*, **12**(5), 630–644.

Gupta, Joyeeta. 2010. A History of International Climate Change Policy. *Wiley Interdisciplinary Reviews: Climate Change*, **1**(5), 636–653.

Hafner-Burton, Emilie Marie, & Montgomery, Alexander H. 2006. Power Positions: International Organizations, Social Networks, and Conflict. *Journal of Conflict Resolution*, **50**(1), 3–27.

Handel, M. 1981. *Weak States in the International System*. Totowa, NJ Frank Cass and Company Limited.

Harris, Paul G. 2009. *World Ethics and Climate Change: From International to Global Justice: From International to Global Justice*. Edinburgh University Press.

Harrison, K. 2007. The Road not Taken: Climate Change Policy in Canada and the United States. *Global Environmental Politics*, **7**(4), 92–117.

Harrison, K. & Sundstrom, L. McIntosh. 2007. The Comparative Politics of Climate Change. *Global Environmental Politics*, **7**(4), 1–18.

Hochstetler, Kathryn & Viola, Eduardo. 2012. Brazil and the Politics of Climate Change: Beyond the Global Commons. *Environmental Politics*, **21**(5), 753–771.

Hoffmann, Matthew. 2011. *Climate Governance at the Crossroads: Experimenting with a Global Response after Kyoto*. Oxford University Press.

Hsiang, S., Kopp, R., Jina, A., Rising, J., Delgado, M., Mohan, S., Rasmussen, D. J., Muir-Wood, R., Wilson, P., Oppenheimer, M., Larsen, K., & Houser, T. 2017. Estimating Economic Damage from Climate Change in the United States. *Science*, **356**(6345), 1362–1369.

Hultman, Nathan. 2011. The Political Economy of Nuclear Energy. *Wiley Interdisciplinary Reviews: Climate Change*, **2**(3), 397–411.

Ikenberry, G. J., Mastanduno, M., & Wohlforth, W. C. 2009. Unipolarity, State Behavior, and Systemic Consequences. *World Politics*, **61**(1): 1–27.

Ingebritsen, Christine, Neumann, Iver, & Gsthl, Sieglinde. 2012. *Small States in International Relations*. University of Washington Press.

Jakobsen, P. V. 2009. Small States, Big Influence: The Overlooked Nordic Influence on the Civilian ESDP. *JCMS: Journal of common market studies*, **47**(1), 81–102.

Javeline, Debra. 2014. The Most Important Topic Political Scientists Are Not Studying: Adapting to Climate Change. *Perspectives on Politics*, **12**(2), 420–434.

Jinnah, Sikina. 2017. Maker, Takers, Shapers, Shakers: Emerging Economies and Normative Engagement in Climate Governance. *Global Governance*, **23**(2), 285–306.

Johnson, T. & Urpelainen, J. 2012. A Strategic Theory of Regime Integration and Separation. *International Organization*, **66**(4), 645–677.

Kahler, Miles. 2013. Rising Powers and Global Governance: Negotiating Change in a Resilient Status Quo. *International Affairs*, **89**(3), 711–729.

Kasa, S., Gullberg, A. T., & Heggelund, G. 2008. The Group of 77 in the International Climate Negotiations: Recent Developments and Future Directions. *International Environmental Agreements: Politics, Law and Economics*, **8**(2), 113–127.

Katzenstein, Peter J. 1985. *Small States in World Markets: Industrial Policy in Europe*. Cornell University Press.

Keohane, R. O. 1969. Lilliputians Dilemmas: Small States in International Politics. *International Organization*, **23**, 291–310.

Keohane, R. O. 2005. *After Hegemony: Cooperation and Discord in the World Political Economy*. Princeton University Press.

Keohane, Robert O. 1971. The Big Influence of Small Allies. *Foreign Policy*, **2**, 161–182.

Kertzer, Joshua D. & Rathbun, Brian C. 2015. Fair is Fair: Social Preferences and Reciprocity in International Politics. *World Politics*, **67**(4), 613–655.

Konisky, David M., Hughes, Llewelyn, & Kaylor, Charles H. 2016. Extreme Weather Events and Climate Change Concern. *Climatic Change*, **134**(4), 533–547.

Koremenos, Barbara, Lipson, Charles, & Snidal, Duncan. 2001. The Rational Design of International Institutions. *International Organization*, **55**(4), 761–799.

Krasner, Stephen D. 1991. Global Communications and National Power: Life on the Pareto Frontier. *Wold Politics*, **43**(3), 336–366.

Lachapelle, Erick & Paterson, Matthew. 2013. Drivers of National Climate Policy. *Climate Policy*, **13**(5), 547–571.

Lee, Donna. 2009. *The Diplomacy of Small States: Between Vulnerability and Resilience*. London: Palgrave Macmillan. Chap. "Bringing an Elephant into the Room: Small African State Diplomacy in the WTO," pages 195–206.

Leebron, David W. 2002. Linkages. *American Journal of International Law*, **96**(1), 5–27.

Leeds, Brett Ashley & Savun, Burcu. 2007. Terminating Alliances: Why do States Abrogate Agreements? *Journal of Politics*, **69**(4), 1118–1132.

Lowe, W., Benoit, K., Mikhaylov, S., & Laver, M. 2011. Scaling Policy Preferences from Coded Political Texts. *Legislative Studies Quarterly*, **36**(1), 123–155.

Lyne, Mona M., Nielson, Daniel L., & Tierney, Michael J. 2006. Who Delegates? Alternative Models of Principals in Development Aid. *Delegation and Agency in International Organizations*, 41–76.

Majeski, Stephen J. & Fricks, Shane. 1995. Conflict and Cooperation in International Relations. *Journal of Conflict Resolution*, **39**, 622–645.

Mansfield, E. D., Milner, H. V., & Rosendorff, B. P. 2000. Free to Trade: Democracies, Autocracies, and International Trade. *American Political Science Review*, **94**(2), 305–321.

Matthews, S. A. 1989. Veto Threats: Rhetoric in a Bargaining Game. *The Quarterly Journal of Economics*, **104**(2), 347–369.

Mayer, F. W. 1992. Managing Domestic Differences in International Negotiations: The Strategic Use of Internal Side-Payments. *International Organization*, **46**(4), 793–818.

McKibben, Heather Elko. 2013. The Effects of Power and Structure on State Bargaining Strategies. *American Journal of Political Science*, **57**(2), 411–427.

Michaelowa, Axel & Michaelowa, Katharina. 2015. Do Rapidly Developing Countries Take Up New Responsibilities for Climate Change Mitigation? *Climatic Change*, **133**(3), 499–510.

Michaelowa, K. & Michaelowa, A. 2012. India as an Emerging Power in International Climate Negotiations. *Climate Policy*, **12**(5), 575–590.

Mills, Evan. 2005. Insurance in a Climate of Change. *Science*, **309**(5737), 1040–1044.

Milner, Helen V. & Kubota, Keiko. 2005. Why The Move to Free Trade? Democracy and Trade Policy in the Developing Countries. *International Organization*, **59**(1), 107–143.

Milner, Helen V. & Rosendorff, B. Peter. 1996. Trade Negotiations, Information and Domestic Politics: The Role of Domestic Groups. *Economics and Politics*, **8**(2), 145–189.

Moravcsik, Andrew. 1998. *The Choice for Europe: Social Purposes and State Power from Messina to Maastricht*. Ithaca, NY: Cornell University Press.

Murdie, A. & Urpelainen, J. 2014. Why Pick on Us? Environmental INGOs and State Shaming as a Strategic Substitute. *Political Studies*, **63**(2), 353–372.

Najam, A., Huq, S., & Sokona, Y. 2003. Climate Negotiations Beyond Kyoto: Developing Countries Concerns and Interests. *Climate Policy*, **3**, 221–231.

Nash, J. 1950. The Bargaining Problem. *Econometrica*, **18**(2), 155–162.

Nordhaus, William D. 2006. *Samuelsonian Economics and the Twenty-First Century*. Oxford: Oxford University Press. Chap. "Paul Samuelson and Global Public Goods."

Nye, J. J. 2004. *Soft Power: The Means to Success in World Politics*. 1st edition. Public Affairs.

O' Fordham, Benjamin. 2011. Who Wants to be a Major Power? Explaining the Expansion of Foreign Policy Ambition. *Journal of Peace Research*, **48**(5), 587–603.

Obradovich, Nick, Tingley, Dustin & Rahwana, Iyad. 2018. Effects of Environmental Stressors on Daily Governance. *Proceedings of the National Academy of Sciences*, **115**(35), 8710–8715.

Okereke, Chukwumerije, Bulkeley, Harriet & Schroeder, Heike. 2009. Conceptualizing Climate Governance Beyond the International Regime. *Global Environmental Politics*, **9**(1), 58–78.

Ourbak, T. & Magnan, A. K. 2018. The Paris Agreement and Climate Change Negotiations: Small Islands, Big Players. *Regional Environmental Change*, **18**(8), 2201–2207.

Panke, Diana. 2010. Small States in the European Union: Structural Disadvantages in EU PolicyMaking and Counter-Strategies. *Journal of European Public Policy*, **17**(6), 799–817.

Panke, Diana. 2013. *Unequal Actors in Equalising Institutions: Negotiations in the United Nations General Assembly*. Houndmills: Palgrave.

Parker, C. F., Karlsson, C., Hjerpe, M. & Linnér, B.-O. 2012. Fragmented Climate Change Leadership: Making Sense of the Ambiguous Outcome of COP-15. *Environmental Politics*, **21**(2), 268–286.

Payne, R. 2001. Persuasion, Frames, and Norm Construction. *European Journal of International Relations*, **7**(1), 37–61.

Prakash, Aseem & Gugerty, Mary Kay. 2010. *Advocacy Organizations and Collective Action*. Cambridge University Press.

Remling, Elisa & Persson, Asa. 2014. Who is Adaptation for? Vulnerability and Adaptation Benefits in Proposals Approved by the UNFCCC Adaptation Fund. *Climate and Development*, **7**(5), 16–34.

Ringius, L., Torvanger, A., & Underdal, A. 2002. Burden Sharing and Fairness Principles in International Climate Policy. *International Environmental Agreements: Politics, Law and Economics*, **2**, 1–22.

Risse, Thomas. 1995. *Bringing Transnational Relations Back in: Non-State Actors, Domestic Structures and International Institutions*. Cambridge University Press.

Risse, Thomas, Ropp, Steve C., & Sikkink, Kathryn (eds). 1999. *The Power of Human Rights: International Norms and Domestic Change*. Cambridge: Cambridge University Press. Chap. "The Socializaton of International Human Rights Norms into Domestic Practices."

Rootes, Christopher. 2008. The First Climate Change Election? The Australian General Election of 24 November 2007. *Environmental Politics*, **17**(3), 473–480.

Rothstein, Robert L. 1968. *Alliances and Small Powers*. New York and London: Columbia University Press.

Rübbelke, Dirk. 2011. International Support of Climate Change Policies in Developing Countries: Strategic, Moral and Fairness Aspects. *Ecological Economics*, **70**(8), 1470–1480.

Schelling, T. C. 1960. *The Strategy of Conflict*. Harvard University Press.

Schneider, Christina. 2009. *Conflict, Negotiations, and EU Enlargement*. Cambridge University Press.

Schneider, Christina J. 2011. Weak States and Institutionalized Bargaining Power in International Organizations. *International Studies Quarterly*, **55**(2): 331–355.

Schneider, G., Finke, D., & Bailer, S. 2010. Bargaining Power in the European Union: An Evaluation of Competing Game-Theoretic Models. *Political Studies*, **58**(1), 85–103.

Schreurs, Miranda A. & Tiberghien, Yves. 2007. Multi-Level Reinforcement: Explaining European Union Leadership in Climate Change Mitigation. *Global Environmental Politics*, 7(4), 19–46.

Schroeder, Heike. 2010. Agency in International Climate Negotiations: The Case of Indigenous Peoples and Avoided Deforestation. *International Environmental Agreements: Politics, Law and Economics*, **10**(4), 317–332.

Schulze, Kai & Tosun, Jale. 2013. External Dimensions of European Environmental Policy: An Analysis of Environmental Treaty Ratification by Third States. *European Journal of Political Research*, **52**(5), 581–607.

Simmons, B. 2009. *Mobilizing for Human Rights: International Law in Domestic Politics*. New York: Cambridge University Press.

Simmons, B. A. & Guzman, A. 2005. Power Plays and Capacity Constraints: The Selection of Defendants in WTO Disputes. *Journal of Legal Studies*, **34**(2), 557–598.

Simmons, Beth. 2000. International Law and State Behavior: Commitment and Compliance in International Monetary Affairs. *American Political Science Review*, **94**(4), 819–835.

Simmons, Beth A., Dobbin, Frank, & Garrett, Geoffrey. 2008. *The Global Diffusion of Markets and Democracy*. Cambridge: Cambridge University Press.

Skovgaard, J. 2013. EU Climate Policy After the Crisis. *Environmental Politics*, **23**(1), 1–17.

Slapin, Jonathan B. 2008. Bargaining Power at Europe's Intergovernmental Conferences: Testing Institutional and Intergovernmental Theories. *International Organization*, **62**(1), 131–162.

Sprinz, D. & Vaahtoranta, T. 1994. The Interest-Based Explanation of International Environmental Policy. *International Organization*, **48**(1), 77–105.

Sprinz, D. F., Bueno de Mesquita, B. & Kallbekken, S. et al. 2016. Predicting Paris: Multi-Method Approaches to Forecast the Outcomes of Global Climate Negotiations. *Politics and Governance*, **4**(3), 172–187.

Sprinz, Detlef F. & Weiss, Martin. 2001. *International Relations and Global Climate Change (Global Environmental Accord: Strategies for Sustainability and Institutional Innovation)*. The MIT Press. Chap. 4. "Domestic Politics and Global Climate Policy."

Steinberg, Richard H. 2002. In the Shadow of Law or Power? Consensus-Based Bargaining and Outcomes in the GATT/WTO. *International Organization*, **56**(2), 339–374.

Stone, Randall W. 2011. *Controlling Institutions: International Organizations and the Global Economy*. Cambridge University Press.

Tallberg, Jonas. 2010. The Power of the Chair: Formal Leadership in International Cooperation. *International Studies Quarterly*, **54**, 241–265.

Thomson, Robert & Stockman, F. N. 2006. *The European Union Decides*. Cambridge University Press. Chap. "Research Design: Measuring Actors' Positions, Saliences and Capabilities." Editors: R. Thomson, F. N. Stockman, C. H. Achen, T. König.

Thomson, Robert, Stockman, Frans N., Achen, Christopher H. & König, Thomas. 2006. *The European Union Decides*. Cambridge University Press.

Tomz, Michael. 2007. Domestic Audience Costs in International Relations: An Experimental Approach. *International Organization*, **61**(4), 821–840.

Tomz, Michael & Weeks, Jessica. 2013. Public Opinion and the Democratic Peace. *American Political Science Review*, **107**(4), 849–865.

Underdal, A. 1980. *The Politics of International Fisheries Managements: The Case of the Northeast Atlantic*. New York, NY: Columbia University Press.

Underdal, A. 2017. Climate Change and International Relations (After Kyoto). *Annual Review of Political Science*, **20**, 169–188.

UNFCCC. 2012. *Submissions from Parties*. https://unfccc.int/process-and-meetings/parties-non-party-stakeholders/parties/archive-of-party-submissions/submissions-from-parties-to-the-cop.

Urpelainen, Johannes. 2011a. The Enforcement-Exploitation Trade-Off in International Cooperation between Weak and Powerful States. *European Journal of International Relations*, **17**(4), 631–653.

Urpelainen, Johannes. 2011b. Technology Investment, Bargaining, and International Environmental Agreements. *International Environmental Agreements: Politics, Law and Economics*, **12**(2), 145–163.

Urpelainen, Johannes & Van de Graaf, Thijs. 2018. United States Non-Cooperation and the Paris Agreement. *Climate Policy*, **18**(7), 839–851.

Vanhala, L. & Hestbaek, C. 2016. Framing Climate Change Loss and Damage in UNFCCC Negotiations. *Global Environmental Politics*, **16**(4), 111–129.

Victor, D. G. 2001. *The collapse of the Kyoto Protocol and the Struggle to Slow Global Warming*. Princeton University Press.

Victor, D. G. 2006. Towards Effective International Cooperation on Climate Change: Numbers, Interests and Institutions. *Global Environmental Politics*, **6**(3), 90–103.

Vihma, Antto, Yacob Mulugetta, & Karlsson-Vinkhuyzen, Sylvia. 2011. Negotiating Solidarity? The G77 through the Prism of Climate Change Negotiations. *Global Change, Peace and Security*, **23**(3), 315–334.

Vital, David. 1967. *The Inequality of States*. New York: Oxford University Press.

von Stein, J. 2008. The International Law and Politics of Climate Change: Ratification of the United Nations Framework Convention and the Kyoto Protocol. *Journal of Conflict Resolution*, **52**(2), 243–268.

Ward, H. 1996. Game Theory and the Politics of Global Warming: the State of Play and Beyond. *Political Studies*, **44**(5), 850–871.

Ward, H., Grundig, F., & Zorick, E. R. 2001. Marching at the Pace of the Slowest: A Model of International Climate-Change Negotiations. *Political Studies*, **49**(3), 438–461.

Weeks, Jessica. 2008. Autocratic Audience Costs: Regime Type and Signaling Resolve. *International Organization*, **62**(1), 35–64.

Weiler, F. 2012. Determinants of Bargaining Success in the Climate Change Negotiations. *Climate Policy*, **12**(5), 552–574.

Wendt, Alexander. 1994. Collective Identity Formation and the International State. *American Political Science Review*, **88**(2), 384–396.

Winkler, H. & Depledge, J. 2018. Fiji-in-Bonn: Will the "Talanoa Spirit" prevail? *Climate Policy*, **18**(2), 141–145.

World Bank. 2012. *World Bank Indicators*. Tech. rept. World Bank.

Acknowledgement

Earlier versions of this Element were circulated at meetings of the European Political Science Association, the Italian Political Science Association, the Southern Political Science Association, and seminars at ETH Zurich, University of Konstanz and University of Essex. I am thankful for comments and feedback from Vincenzo Bove, Alexandra Hennessy, Katharina Holzinger, Gerald Schneider, Ken Scheve, Florian Weiler, the Cambridge University Press Elements editors Jon Pevehouse and Tanja Börzel, as well as the anonymous reviewers. I am grateful to Emily Helms for research assistance, the Deutscher Akademischer Austauschdienst (DAAD) for providing resources to start the project, and the University of Essex for providing resources to finish it. Finally, I am very thankful to my family for trusting my writing capabilities and to Florian Kern for giving me space, time and energy to tackle this project.

Cambridge Elements $\equiv$

International Relations

Jon C. W. Pevehouse
University of Wisconsin–Madison

Jon C. W. Pevehouse is the Vilas Distinguished Achievement Professor of Political Science at the University of Wisconsin–Madison. He has published numerous books and articles in IR in the fields of international political economy, international organizations, foreign policy analysis, and political methodology. He is a former editor of the leading IR field journal, *International Organization*.

Tanja A. Börzel
The Free University of Berlin

Tanja A. Börzel is the Professor of political science and holds the Chair for European Integration at the Otto-Suhr-Institute for Political Science, Freie Universität Berlin. She holds a PhD from the European University Institute, Florence, Italy. She is coordinator of the Research College "The Transformative Power of Europe", as well as the FP7-Collaborative Project "Maximizing the Enlargement Capacity of the European Union" and the H2020 Collaborative Project "The EU and Eastern Partnership Countries: An Inside-Out Analysis and Strategic Assessment". She directs the Jean Monnet Center of Excellence "Europe and Its Citizens".

Edward D. Mansfield
University of Pennsylvania

Edward D. Mansfield is the Hum Rosen Professor of Political Science, University of Pennsylvania. He has published well over 100 books and articles in the area of international political economy, international security, and international organizations. He is Director of the Christopher H. Browne Center for International Politics at the University of Pennsylvania and former program co-chair of the American Political Science Association.

About the Series

Cambridge Elements in International Relations publishes original research on key topics in the field. The series includes manuscripts addressing international security, international political economy, international organizations, and international relations theory. Our objective is to publish cutting edge research that engages crucial topics in each of these issue areas, especially multi-method research that may yield longer studies than leading journals in the field will accommodate.

Cambridge Elements ☰

International Relations

Elements in the Series

Weak States at Global Climate Negotiations
Federica Genovese

9781108790901

A full series listing is available at: www.cambridge.org/EIR

Printed in the United States
By Bookmasters